~Paul~
Thank you for bei.... ...d and
a willing partic...

MW00452845

...uly

A THIRST
FOR THE
Infinite

JUDY LLOYD

Print ISBN: 978-1-54399-531-2

eBook ISBN: 978-1-54399-532-9

Preface

C.S.Lewis's words on becoming perfect really resonated with me as I read his statement that, "If we wish to be rational, not now and then, but constantly, we must pray for the gift of faith". This nonfiction book is an approach to understanding life's jolting events as our beliefs are being challenged by a variety of adversities. Remaining faithful and prayerful in the midst of the turmoil guarantees we experience spiritual graduate school. This book is dedicated to my family members and friends who have enriched and blessed my life when my soul was thirsting for the infinite.

TABLE OF CONTENTS

Chapter One

COURAGE TO GRIEVE

The powerful hand of death will touch each of us more than once as we experience our earthly sojourn. It may be a brushing of our shoulder as it approaches an acquaintance or it may be a full hand shake as it visits someone we cherish. The realization that we will not be left comfortless as we petition for solace is easy to acknowledge beforehand. However, in the midst of sorrow, questions may arise that are both confusing and troubling. "Why did this happen to me?" "Why must I experience disappointment?" "When will my heart stop aching?" The issue of life and death is an issue that is complex and difficult to comprehend.

For example, imagine the delight felt by both father and mother immediately following the birth of their beautiful baby girl; she is considered a rainbow baby. Her parents have eagerly anticipated her birth while also being cautious with their feelings. They had experienced a still-birth several years previous to her arrival and understood the possibility that this infant might also be stillborn. These parents recognized that the deeper their well of pain from their previous experience the greater their joy will be as their lives are blessed. In their wisdom they would never have deliberately invited pain into their lives and they would not avoid risks in order to avoid the possibility of pain.

Now, imagine their joy when after months of eager anticipation their baby has been delivered without any concerns. Cradling her newborn in her arms the mother feels immense relief as her baby wraps her tiny fingers around her mother's pinky. Peering at her mother through curious eyes, the baby suddenly arches her back as though she is proclaiming relief at having escaped the cramped quarters of the womb. Her baby smile is as sweet as the fresh jasmine and her fair skin appears to glow. Noticing that the tiny tuft of hair on the top of her baby's head is as golden as the noonday sun the mother is completely spellbound and realizes she will love her baby through-out all eternity. In celebration of this blessed event amazing food begins to arrive at their home delivered by extended family and friends. Gifts are also delivered to the delight of the family and prayers of gratitude are offered by many.

One quiet evening a close friend approaches the mother of the newborn and makes inquiries regarding the family's current good fortune. She is eager to know if the new babe will somehow dissolve the pain resulting from the previous birth of the stillborn baby. The mother explains that some things are beyond describing. She relates that losing her other baby was a horrendous ordeal and couldn't possibly be fully understood except by others who had experienced a similar trial. While she remains grateful for all the support her family received during their initial loss, she felt the greatest support had come from parents who had experienced a similar loss. Those parents had offered suggestions that they knew to be helpful. As these new parents grieved their loss they had been by encouraged to understand that human resilience is amazing and to recognize their pain as their teacher, not their enemy. The realization that other parents with dead children were able to cope was the reassurance both she and her husband needed at the time of their loss. It was very important for them to understand that they would survive the suffocating feelings they were going through. Hope was definitely beginning to appear on the horizon because other parents offered words that came not from schooling but from experience. With that hope came the courage to risk another pregnancy.

A time for reflection is a necessity as one learns to maneuver through the ebb tides of life. Occasionally with the ebb tide sorrow is uncovered and as it emerges from beneath its semi-translucent shell which has been its hiding place, one must willingly approach one's sorrow. Approaching sorrow with certain expectations helps a grieving person to avoid flooding his/her days with the waters of a rip tide. Realizing that the greatest battles ever fought are not within the churning waters of a riptide but within the confines of one's own heart, allowing the waves of grief to wash over oneself is a necessity. At the same time, taking the first steps away from the shell of mourning and back into the land of the living is essential in gaining solace. As one refuses to bury their grief, remaining gentle with oneself is imperative.

Reflecting on King David's response to the death of his beloved son brings wisdom to bereaved parents. As I studied his response to the loss of his son I better understood my own response to the loss of our son. As King David observed his son near death he chose to turn from his diet of plenty and began fasting while also turning to sackcloth. He was hopeful that his sacrifices would bring support to the child he dearly loved. However, this was not to be the case. After seven days the child died in spite of having received the best medical attention available. King David became aware of his son's death through the whisperings of his servants. They hesitated to approach him fearful of his response. Once David sought affirmation from his servants that his son was indeed dead, he washed, anointed himself, changed his clothing and went unto the house of the Lord to worship. Then returning to his home he broke his fast. His servants were confused with David's response to his son's death. He wisely advised them that he had made every effort to assure his son would live through weeping, fasting and seeking the grace of God. However his son was dead and now he must return to the living. While his response was steeped in wisdom, some parents including myself, require a lengthier process in which to learn and grow.

Speaking from experience I understand the reality that as a bereaved parent it feels like I have violated a natural law through outliving my child. After the loss of our son, it would take months for me to realize on an internal level that life must go on. During those months, I came to realize that grief was an unwanted visitor who wouldn't stop pounding on my door. My first experience with grief had come when President Kennedy was assassinated. I was sixteen years old and walking the hallways of high school when other students burst into tears and related the devastating news. As a nation, we observed Kennedy's death, his funeral and his family's reactions to his death from a distance, specifically through television. The first lady was a perfect model for living a stoic lifestyle. I believe the pressure she must have felt to "carry on" was unimaginable.

I had been raised in a very stoic family and didn't realize the courage it takes to grieve. I cannot emphasize enough that unending grief is the grief that has not been stared fully in the face. With that action one can alleviate the pain through developing a balance between laughing and crying. The process of grieving is different for each person; this is an incredibly important realization in a couple ship when a child is lost. Unfortunately, sometimes a spouse may feel revulsion for their companion rather than sympathy at a time that sympathy is most needed. Especially if they believe their spouse is demonstrating too little control. Some parents are able to maintain a strong union as they fight for their child's life together. Long, restless nights in hospital rooms can seem endless. Remaining supportive of one another while maintaining vigil over their little one may appear practical and easy enough to do. And yet during a concentrated period of worry about their ill child couples often don't understand the need to remain focused on keeping their lines of communication open. Venting their annoyances with one another over everyday irritants is imperative in order to avoid the development of an emotional volcano resulting in a major eruption. Rather than ignoring or overlooking the ordinary irritants it is wise to discuss any irritants within twenty four hours of their occurrence. If a spouse is too angry to discuss something in the moment it is happening they can allow a cooling down period to take place with the realization a discussion will occur within the allotted twenty four hours.

Understanding that the emotional and physical strain on grieving parents can be over-whelming it is important to recognize that planning their child's funeral does not need to become an additional burden. When our son died, we were exhausted and numb. It was very helpful that we were engaged in a religion that recognized traditional burial customs and we had already begun making plans months before his death. Tenderly and carefully we had involved him in some of the planning. For friends who had lost their children to the same disease this was not an option. Their burial customs varied according to their beliefs and we made every attempt to realize their needs were different than ours. Sensitivity to all customs can bring solace at a time when it is most needed. While we found comfort in ordering red, white and blue flowers for our son's memorial service another culture might find the idea of fresh flowers very strange as the deceased will neither smell nor see the flowers. Also, some cultures may find placing fresh food at the casket of the deceased comforting as the food is placed as an offering to the deceased even though it will never be tasted by them.

Weeks, months and years after the death of our son, I continued to retain an overall memory of being surrounded by family and friends who wanted to support and cushion us in our loss. I remain eternally grateful for their efforts and the time they gave us out of their lives. I also remember insisting that our son's siblings be present with us at his funeral. Our little daughter was still a toddler and having her present rather than apart from our family was imperative to both my husband and myself. Our seven year old son was grief stricken with the loss of his brother and we felt he needed to experience the love and support from our community as much as we did. We did have family members who insisted they remain at home with our children during the funeral service. While we understood their urgency to be helpful, we remained determined to have our children close to us.

After the death of our daughter I was firm in my resolve that there truly is no right or wrong when a family is grieving the loss of a child. For many families unique circumstances arise. When a close friend and her family had to make a move to a different part of the country, she insisted their daughter's casket be moved with them. Her greatest comfort came when sitting at her daughter's grave and she couldn't imagine being denied this opportunity. Her actions to me demonstrated that grief is not automatically shut off after months or even years; for many it is a long term anguish.

There is a technique created by William James over a hundred years ago. This technique can be especially beneficial to someone who feels unable to move beyond their grief. It is the process of acting like you want to do something, even though you may not feel like doing it. While it is easy to isolate and abandon important everyday routines when grief comes knocking, that is a devastating path to take. Grief can be depleting and create pre-occupation that is exhausting. Also, the closer we were to the deceased, the more havoc the loss creates. Each individual we love brings unique experiences to our lives. The loss of the person and those experiences may intensify our feelings of loneliness. To regain one's motivation for life, it is helpful to begin your day with prayer, in spite of not "feeling like it". Seek the Holy Spirit for comfort remembering that the road less traveled may be a hard one but it is made much easier by the companionship of the Holy Spirit. Then visualize yourself showering, dressing, and approaching other family members and friends. Once this process is complete begin the activities, remaining focused on healthy desires. Also it's important to take small steps while attempting to return to a healthy pattern of living. Perhaps baking a favorite dessert rather than purchasing one already made would be helpful but not over-whelming. While physically engaging in the process, feelings of encouragement and hope will come. This "act as if" principle has been used extensively within all motivational change work including recovery from addictions, reduction of anxiety, weight management and many other tedious tasks. When making honest efforts, the use of this principle can help to restore confidence and courage to one's life.

Developing an understanding of the difference between normal guilt and neurotic guilt is paramount to living in peace after suffering a major loss. It is hard to imagine that a parent would not feel any guilt with the loss of a child. The "if only's" are a natural part of the grief process and can be expected. However, in order to avoid alienation from Heavenly Father one must strive to comprehend any unresolved guilt and other misunderstood emotions. For example maintaining vigilance over a dying person can be very draining. Perhaps a person leaves their "post" to get some much needed rest only to have their loved one die while they are away from the bedside. This situation is not uncommon and it can create neurotic guilt that might result in a variety of health problems. Approaching someone professionally for guidance allows support that may be necessary to ensure a person has the capacity to return to their daily activities.

 Feelings of inadequacy are so very common when illness strikes. As people valiantly struggle for life while dealing with a life-threatening disease, they often are faced with the need to understand their own emotional, physical and spiritual needs. Remembering that sickness is not comfortable for anyone, there are practical ways to reach out and support a friend in need. Too often a person may be enjoying a happy productive life that is suddenly interrupted with a dreaded diagnosis. Remaining open and present to their feelings is all that is needed. One doesn't have to say anything; demonstrating love and concern while perhaps confessing that you don't know what to say may be the most useful approach. And it may create a deeper level of friendship and trust at a time it is most needed.

Should a person allow themselves to express negative emotions when they have received difficult news regarding their own health or the health of a loved one? This question brings the story of Job to my mind. He complained bitterly about his circumstances apparently to anyone who would listen. Some who heard his words were good friends and they encouraged repentance on his part as he expressed his disappointments. At the same time, Job was adamant that "Though he slay me, yet will I trust in him" (Job 13:15). He went on to express his powerful belief that "He also shall be my salvation" (Job 13:16). Job clearly understood that Heavenly Father's love is unconditional and he remains with us right where we are in each given moment. Allowing us the dignity to have our own feelings, we can rest assured that we will not be abandoned in our greatest time of need. This knowledge will help a person who is suffering avoid the development of neurotic guilt.

I find it important to be clear regarding offers of support when contacting a person who is suffering emotionally or physically. Making a blanket offer such as, "let me know if there is anything I can do", means just that. "Anything I can do" covers a lot of territory and it is important that any offers be realistic and honest. Remaining flexible is also important. Perhaps I have already created a plan of action to support someone and call that person to schedule my visit. They may surprise me with a different plan. Remaining flexible will help me avoid building negative feelings such as irritation or frustration.

William Cowper stated, "Knowledge is proud that it knows so much; wisdom is humble it knows no more". All the knowledge that we have and can obtain regarding grief still does not give us enough wisdom when we are blinded by grief. As I mentioned previously, remaining gentle on ourselves and others is imperative as we journey through this sometimes complicated life.

In addition, learning to allow the Savior to be our shield of protection against grief, disappointment and spiritual pain requires willingness. This allowance is not an instant achievement however. And just like the beginning of a race, healing has its starting point. Our Savior in his desire to succor us can work around our inadequacies as we demonstrate our willingness and desires. No matter how deeply entrenched our grief may be each of us can begin the process of healing as we focus on the true desires of our hearts while remembering we are involved in a process. Also while we may mentally have a sincere desire for healing, emotionally we may lack the strength to pursue our desires. Praying for the needed strength to engage in the healing process may be the beginning point for some. In the meantime, we can rest assured that as we begin this process the adversary will be just as determined to undermine our efforts.

There is a story that has been repeated many times in the twelve step community. It begins with a man who is returning home from a day of demanding work. As he walks the familiar path he has tread for many years, he encounters a snake curled up in the middle of the roadway, completely frozen. The man realizes by the color of the snake that its bite is deadly. At the same time, the man feels compassion and is amazed at the beauty of the snake. With the combined feelings of awe and empathy the man chooses to gently pick the snake up and carry it home. Upon entering his cabin and building a warm fire, the man places the snake upon the hearth to help it begin thawing. As he carefully places a bowl of warm milk in front of the snake, it strikes with a deadly blow. As the man lay dying from the snake's venom he cries out in agony, "How could you do this to me? I was attempting to save your life!" The snake hisses, "You knew I was poison when you picked me up". In his desire to be helpful the man chose to be oblivious to the fact that the snake could possibly strike and kill him. He had been beguiled by the snake.

Satan and his beguiling ways are the influence behind the opposition to the work of Heavenly Father. Our Savior admonished us in Matthew 6:24 to understand that, "No man can serve two masters: for he will hate the one, and love the other; or else he will hold to the one, and despise the other. Ye cannot serve God and mammon." Clearly Satan would have us disbelieve and disregard God's commandments. It is obvious that we must strive daily to grow spiritually in order to discern all the forms of evil that exist in today's world. For example, in many parts of our country abortion has become socially accepted. Abortion clinics have become prevalent as abortion has become a common practice. Because human life is a sacred gift from God, elective abortion for personal or social convenience goes against the commandment, "Thou shalt not kill". Mother Teresa was a Yugoslavian nun who cared for the poorest and most destitute people of India for many years. Her powerful spirit spoke volumes as she delivered her message that the greatest proof of selfishness is abortion. She demonstrated through her actions that any country that accepts abortion is not teaching its people to love, but to use any form of violence needed in order to get what they desire. There is wisdom in remembering that anywhere abortion is allowed to flourish, we will be witness to the unraveling of the fabric of human society.

It has been my experience that answers to prayers seldom arrive as quickly as we would desire. The adversary works to use this postponement against us. Persisting with our petitions to our Heavenly Father may become difficult as prayers become more like anxious pleas. Sometimes a change in one's attitude is necessary in order to remain open to God's help. His divine love and understanding of our needs evolves from an eternal perspective. Realizing Satan will not be able to defeat us on the battleground of prayer brings us the reassurance we need during the most trying of times.

Traveling over the mountain passes in southern Colorado offered us the opportunity to realize how imperative it is that we not cross over the lines that clearly marked the side of the road we needed to be on. Several times forceful rainstorms including loud claps of thunder and brilliant flashes of lightning made it almost impossible to determine which side of the road we were on. Our deepest desire was to avoid a head-on crash with another vehicle or a dive into the canyon resulting in a catastrophe.

Understanding that there is a line of demarcation dividing good from evil allows us to remain on the well- defined side of the Lord's. As we choose to do so, we are assured that we will receive help in our daily struggles and spiritual battles. A study of ancient Israel demonstrates just how important armor can be. The breastplate was a central part of the Roman soldier's armor, providing protection for the torso where the vital organs are found. Without his breastplate a soldier would be asking for death. We read in Proverbs 11:4, "Riches do not profit in the day of wrath, but righteousness delivers from death". Understanding the war between the Lord and Satan is for the faithfulness of the heart, our hearts deserve spiritual protection. Satan's fiery darts of temptation intended to wound one's heart will be deflected as we honor and obey our Savior.

Our Savior suffered pains, afflictions and temptations of every kind in order to be perfect in his ability to empathize with us. Therefore there is no human condition which he cannot comprehend. He understands our afflictions and infirmities, has deep love and compassion for us and knows exactly how to help us. Remembering that our Savior cried out to his Father for help gives us permission to follow that divine example. We have several favorite pictures of our Savior in our home. These pictures serve as reminders of our commitments we have made to remain as steadfast disciples. It's all about determining what holds our attention.

Chapter Two

KISS OF DEATH

Closing the clasp on my necklace I experienced waves of gratitude for the words engraved upon it; "A Family's Love Is Nature's Masterpiece". Turning to the corridors of my memory, experiences that broadened my vision and expanded my soul are vivid. Strolling those corridors, meditating on the lives of people who lived and loved with fire in their souls, I notice Cynthia peeking out at me. In her precocious and playful fashion, she giggles while giving me a thumbs- up. Oh! How I yearn for one more opportunity to brush her golden hair and listen to her "counsel" her younger sister Amanda. After thirty-five years, I continue to imagine her as an impish eight year old singing lullabies to her baby dolls. At the same time, I envision her brother Roger as a handsome young man, fully grown, towering over me.

Roger was our first born. Before his birth, Stan and I agreed we would be happy with either a son or daughter. With his birth, we marveled at the miracle of life. Initially, Roger was a peaceful and contented infant. One evening, several days before Christmas I carefully wrapped him in blankets to keep him warm and cozy. The night had approached with the promise of a light snow. We were looking forward to our drive through neighborhoods, admiring the abundant and amazing Christmas displays. Settling into the passenger's seat, I loosened the blankets around Roger. Looking into his eyes, my love for him was boundless. Leaning forward to kiss his forehead, I was a bit startled to discover he tasted of salt. Having been the second oldest in a family of nine children, I realized none of my siblings had ever tasted salty. Little did I realize what that kiss meant. It would be weeks before I would hear it referred to as the "kiss of death".

Within a few weeks of Roger's birth, he developed a harsh cough. He was also experiencing considerable diarrhea. Because work took him out of town each week, Stan's parents encouraged me to stay with them in their home. Feeling relieved with their offer, I packed up bags for Roger and myself and soon found us settled comfortably into their home.

"Did you hear back from the pediatrician's office?" my mother-in-law inquired early one morning. "I have an appointment scheduled for later today" was my response. Driving to that appointment several hours later, I fervently prayed for answers; clearly Roger was not thriving. As the pediatrician examined Roger, he expressed his upset with me. "How could you have taken your newborn out into the community at such a young age", he demanded to know. Imagine my dismay as he diagnosed Roger with whooping cough and had him admitted to the hospital. Gratefully, I was allowed to remain with our infant son. Silently, I begged Roger's forgiveness as his tiny scalp was injected with an IV. Faithfully, I phoned friends and family seeking prayers for our little one.

Following two weeks of hospitalization Roger was released from the pediatrics unit. While he had responded to the antibiotics and IV solution for hydration, he remained underweight. Driving him home, I promised him he would not have to experience another hospital stay. Yet even as I made that commitment, I felt a silent foreboding. The foreboding was so powerful, it felt like a heavy gray cloud warning of a dark storm approaching.

One morning while relaxing in the home of my in-laws I began reading the Albuquerque Journal. Feeling drawn to an article about a recent convention held in Albuquerque, I called out to my mother-in-law and proceeded to share the article with her. The focus of the convention was on the progress being made in the diagnosis and treatment of Cystic Fibrosis. Reading the symptoms outlined in the article, that gray cloud that had been tenaciously hovering above my head released a torrential downpour. Quickly recovering from my heavy cloud of despair and subsequent "drenching" I scribbled a note with the name of the clinic on it.

Although Roger had only been with us for a brief few weeks, his young spirit seemed to resonate with mine. It felt as though we both were experiencing a double-edged sword. Joy and sorrow wrapped up in one exquisite package. By the time Roger had reached the tender age of six weeks, he was back in the hospital in Farmington. His horrendous cough was back and he was not gaining weight. He also continued to have bulky, foul-smelling bowel movements.

A mother's guilt is incomprehensible when her child is ill. Following several weeks of hospitalization, we were allowed to take Roger home. The pediatrician had continued with his shaming and impatient behavior. I felt an alarming need to run from him. But where would I run to? I became prayerful, depending on the Holy Spirit to guide me. Almost immediately, I felt compelled to call the clinic in Albuquerque.

As I made the call we were encouraged to bring Roger in as soon as possible. Speaking with Stan, he stated he wanted to drive us. Fortunately, Stan's employer was building a power line locally and he was supportive of Stan taking a day off. We would make the four hour drive to Albuquerque the following day. Feeling hopeful we were able to relax and sleep soundly that night. It was still dark when the alarm clock rang the following morning. Turning off the alarm I glanced quickly outside relieved to see a blanket of brightly sparkling stars in the clear sky. Our drive into the big city would be made easier with a highway free of ice and snow.

Grateful for an uneventful drive, we arrived at the hospital on schedule. Taking a moment to collect our thoughts and utter a prayer it was with renewed anticipation that we approached the hospital staff. We were directed to the pediatric unit where we were introduced to the physician who would bring us needed answers.

"I have made arrangements to admit Roger to the hospital", the pediatrician explained as he described the procedures that would take place. Soon after Roger's admission a cheerful nurse took our baby son to another part of the hospital. She explained x-rays would be taken, an IV started and a sweat test conducted. As Roger was whisked away, my entire being felt like mush. Attempting to focus, I explained to Stan that I must be experiencing an anxiety attack. He drew me close and shared his understanding. As we consoled one another, we continued to hope for a miracle.

After what seemed like an endless amount of time, the nurse returned with our infant son lying in a small crib she was pushing. He was wailing, clearly feeling a need to be soothed. Carefully picking him up, Roger snuggled into my arms. His sobs slowly turned to little whimpers, followed by silence as I sang him a lullaby. I could sense rather than see the pediatrician approaching us. He invited us into an office located on the pediatrics unit. Stan and I settled into comfortable chairs as I continued to soothe our infant son.

"The sweat test has confirmed my suspicions", explained the doctor. "Roger has Cystic Fibrosis. We will release him as soon as we get him stabilized. His prognosis is guarded as he is a very sick cystic. Also, arrangements have also been made for you to remain with your baby." Depression settled like road dust on me as we agreed Stan would go back home to work and I would remain with Roger. To lift my spirits, Stan stated he would return to us over the weekend to bring me clean clothing and lots of hugs. He would make that trip twice as we would be at Bataan Hospital for three weeks.

When we did take Roger home, we felt armed with both information and tools that would enhance our little man's life. Instead of breast feeding he would be offered a formula that was pre-digested. Raising his crib from the floor on one end allowed postural drainage in his lungs as he slept slanted downwards. Roger would also sleep in a clear tent of plastic that had a mist being released into it. The mist would create an environment that would help the mucous in his lungs remain more fluid.

We realized we had so much to discover about this dreaded disease. Learning that Cystic Fibrosis is a genetic, chronic, progressive and frequently fatal disease we felt confused as neither of us were aware of any family history or experience to refer to. We were taught that with Cystic Fibrosis a mutation in a gene changes a protein that requires the movement of salt in and out of cells. The result is thick, sticky mucus in the respiratory, digestive and reproductive systems. With the thick mucus, symptoms that are common include wheezing, shortness of breath and a persistent cough that produces a thick phlegm. Cystic Fibrosis also creates increased salt in the sweat which explained why Roger tasted of salt early on. We learned that many different defects can occur in the gene. The type of gene mutation is associated with the severity of the condition. Also, children need to inherit one copy of the gene from each parent in order to have the disease. If children inherit only one copy, they won't develop cystic fibrosis, but will be carriers and possibly pass the gene to their own children. Obviously, Roger had inherited a copy of the gene from each of us. We also learned that Cystic Fibrosis is one of the most common genetic diseases affecting about one in every twenty-five hundred babies born in the United States. It is also most common among Caucasians and Hispanics and is rarely found in people of African or Asian descent.

Continuing our journey with Roger we came to learn that many feelings are wrapped up in a life-threatening illness. Those feelings include sadness, guilt, anger, frustration, and helplessness. The roller coaster ride of emotions can be over-whelming. I found myself experiencing difficulty swallowing food, sleeping or concentrating. Eventually a very wise woman offered me counsel. She stated, "I have learned to pray to Heavenly Father at bedtime. I ask him to take my difficult emotions from me for the night. I commit to take back in the morning whatever he wants me to have. Then sleep will come and in the days that follow I will learn whatever lessons are being offered me." With time and practice I was able to follow her enlightening counsel and the hollow pain knotting my stomach began to diminish. I realized I was moving past my mountain of over-whelming feelings. Other prayers were answered following Roger's diagnosis.

While Stan had been working three jobs to make ends meet he was now offered an apprenticeship with the local utilities. We would be blessed with adequate income as well as health insurance.

As the weeks and months flew by, Roger continued to surprise everyone with his tenacity and courage. Experiencing numerous stays in the hospital, he always found a younger child to offer his friendship to. It was like a temporary adoption, easing his desire for a sibling. During one of those hospital visits in Farmington, a young Navajo boy was admitted to the pediatrics unit. He had been kicked in the head by a horse. His parents lived on the reservation and would have to return to their community for work and to care for their other children. It was apparent they were having a difficult time leaving their little one. Roger approached them rather cautiously, pulling a red wagon behind him while I guided his IV pole. While they didn't speak English they understood Roger's interest in pulling their little one in the wagon. They willingly obliged Roger by placing their son in the wagon and we were off. I stayed beside the wagon guarding its precious cargo while maneuvering Roger's IV pole. Other little ones would join our entourage, clapping and singing as we made our way down the corridors.

Staff members from the hospitals in Albuquerque and Farmington developed friendships with Roger as well. He was especially grateful for a specific phlebotomist at the Albuquerque hospital who was skilled in drawing blood gases. This particular test measures the acidity (pH) and the levels of oxygen and carbon dioxide in the blood from an artery. For a youngster who has only a few pounds of weight on his young body, going into the wrist for this draw was especially painful; the experience would be less painful if the phlebotomist "had the gift of the draw". One year during the Halloween season Roger was hospitalized in Albuquerque. His favorite phlebotomist appeared in a costume that was very fitting. He was dressed as a vampire. Their antics together were quite amusing as Roger held onto his neck and begged the "vampire" to please go away. Laughing, the phlebotomist reached for Roger's wrist and had the draw completed as quickly and as painlessly as possible.

Roger also loved to play tricks on his respiratory therapists. His rubber snake could be found dangling from a cupboard or crawling from beneath his bed. He especially enjoyed sharing a favorite joke with the hospital staff and any visitors. Asking each of them how to catch a unique rabbit and watching for their puzzled expression he would laughingly respond, "You neek up on it!" I'm not clear how he chose his favorite football team, but Roger definitely was a Dallas Cowboy fan. When he was hospitalized during football season, you could find any number of staff members hanging out in his room with him, cheering and complaining. Roger really enjoyed his Dallas Cowboys jacket which he wore to and from the hospital.

While the hospital food was nothing to write home about, it was ample and nutritious. Of course, the patients had the opportunity to daily choose from a menu with several options on it. After a few days of hospitalization, I could tell that Roger could use a meal meant to delight his palate. If he were hospitalized in Farmington, it was easy to call friends or family for "back-up". However, when he was hospitalized in Albuquerque our choices were limited. Imagine our delight and gratitude one day when several of his nurses from the Philippines presented him with the most aromatic meal we had ever experienced! It was obvious several types of herbs and spices had been used to create the exotic vegetable and meat meal. The main dish was accompanied with a delightful mound of fragrant rice. The sauce used to create the meal was rich with flavor being both creamy and tangy. The nurses made ample servings sharing the joy with me and Stan. We were so very impressed with their thoughtfulness and fantastic food. Over the years to come, these nurses would continue to bless us with their culinary skills. With their direction, I bought a wok and began creating my own family favorites at home.

Roger was very clever when it came to playing chess. He had a 1776 chess game that we would sometimes take with us when he was hospitalized. While he didn't play with staff members, they appeared impressed by his level of skill at playing the game. Quite often he would have me in checkmate before I knew what was happening. He initially played chess with my brother Paul who lived in California. This brother drove out to visit us one summer in a hearse that he had converted into quite "the ride". It was painted candy apple red and had a very comfortable interior.

At this time in his life my brother was attending the University of California, Berkeley and appeared to be living the carefree lifestyle of a hippy wearing his blonde hair shoulder length. Wanting to be helpful he offered to drive me to the drugstore to pick up medications for Roger. Arriving at the drugstore, my brother remained standing outside of his vehicle, enjoying the fresh air and beauty of the morning while I completed my errand. As he relaxed, leaning against his "ride" a man emerged from his pick-up and pointing his finger at my brother, this man began slapping a very large flashlight against his thigh. Apparently he felt threatened by my brother's hippy appearance and had the need to send him a message. Emerging from the drugstore I observed what was happening. Alarmed I rushed over to my brother. He quickly assured me there would be no problems. While he was amused by the situation I found it to be rather sad. I had grown up with my brother and knew him to be a very loving man. I also knew his physical strength and that he was skilled in the martial arts. Apparently my brother believed strongly in the Biblical system of martial arts. This system is found in the first verse of the fifteenth chapter of Proverbs: "A soft answer turneth away wrath". As my brother remained calm with the threats being directed at him, the man realized he would find no foe in this parking lot.

Chapter Three

RENEWED FAITH

Eventually Stan and I began entertaining thoughts of adding another child to our family. Initially, we chose to ignore the thoughts, realizing it was neither a logical or practical idea. The risk of giving birth to another child with Cystic Fibrosis had to be considered. Hoping for a miracle, I considered the life of one of my favorite poets, Henry Wadsworth Longfellow. This man is an excellent example of an individual who remained faithful and optimistic in spite of life's many challenges. Through-out the years a variety of people have discovered the words he wrote offered both hope and inspiration. Longfellow had the respect of many great men and women of his time as well. It is reported he was able to put his friends and others at ease sometimes using kindly humor to keep the conversation light and flowing. He was admired for his charm and humility often speaking with a soft voice and demonstrating a sweet temper. Life is difficult and can throw many curves at a person. And life for Longfellow was filled with sharp curves. He and his first wife Mary had the opportunity to travel together, eventually embarking on a tour of Scandinavian and

European countries. Tragically, while on this trip, Longfellow's wife experienced a miscarriage and died. Longfellow then poured himself into his writing and teaching to deal with his grief. His words encouraged one to live a life of action while avoiding the possibility of being driven by fear.

According to historical accounts it would take seven years before Longfellow would remarry. Together he and his new wife welcomed five children into their home. Longfellow wrote several significant poems during this time, and by 1860 he had found wealth and world-wide fame. In 1861, he had been given honorary degrees at Oxford and Cambridge. He had also been extended an invitation to Windsor Castle by Queen Victoria. In spite of all the favorable circumstances in his life, sorrowfully tragedy struck again. While lighting a match, Longfellow's second wife's clothing was ignited and she would die as a result of the severe burns her body suffered. Longfellow, in an effort to save his wife, was burned on the face. He now found shaving nearly impossible due to the burns he experienced. This resulted in him growing his flowing white beard out of necessity.

Following the pain and sorrow of such a devastating loss, more despair was to visit Longfellow's life. The civil war broke out with fury and major destruction. Longfellow described how he felt the war tear at the very fiber of his being. In time, his oldest son was wounded on the battlefield. The young man was sent home to his father who would assist in his healing. During this time Longfellow lived with the haunting question, "where is the peace?" He appeared desperate to find solace. Reading about Longfellow and all he endured his words resonated with me and I came to realize how a constant diet of dismay can reach deep within the soul, creating a yearning for answers. With his questions Longfellow again turned to writing. As he sat with pen in hand, he heard the ringing of Christmas bells. Eventually, the prose he created would become a favored Christmas hymn, "I Heard the Bells on Christmas Day". Enjoying this hymn and in turn studying Longfellow's life, I was reminded that God is not dead, does not sleep and is very aware of our circumstances. With this encouragement and continued prayer I found renewed faith.

With renewed faith, I encouraged Stan to please consider adding another child to our family. He and I then agreed to remain prayerful regarding this desire, as there were definite risks involved. A few months later we were enjoying a favorite meal when we announced to Roger that we were expecting a baby. He was thrilled and began immediately asking questions. I encouraged him to realize that we had no idea whether it would be a girl or boy, and that the baby most likely wouldn't have Cystic Fibrosis. I also explained that we are sometimes confused with feelings that we are having. It can be difficult to determine if one is feeling fear or excitement. Roger quickly stated that he was so excited. The conversation continued beyond the evening meal. Our home was filled with joy.

Several months into my pregnancy, I awoke one morning to find Stan experiencing excruciating pain. The previous evening we had concluded he might be catching the flu as he had been nauseous and feverish. However, we were both alarmed with the pain he was feeling. It couldn't be his appendix. It had been removed unexpectedly when he was sixteen. Stan agreed that we should drop Roger off at his parents' home and drive him to the emergency room. We moved quickly and within the half hour the physician on duty in the emergency room was offering Stan an explanation.

"You have a kidney stone, we'll admit you to the hospital for hydration, observation and pain management. The stone will pass and you will be just fine." Within the part of my brain referred to as the "adaptive unconscious", I began to feel an intuitive shockwave. The diagnosis didn't explain the fever Stan was experiencing. Because I felt so uneasy with this course of action, I turned to a medical person who would be immediately available and I knew I could trust. She was a nurse's aide in pediatrics and would be on that unit.

Marie was a sprite of a woman with boundless energy. One moment she might be consoling a screaming infant and the next she would be working on an infiltrated IV. She was also a no nonsense type of person and was deeply committed to the care of her young patients. Seeking her out, I quickly described Stan's symptoms to her. She patted me gently on the back and agreed I might want a second opinion. She then advised me to consult with the urologist who had just moved into our community. She believed he might be making hospital rounds as we spoke. Following her counsel I quickly sought support from this particular physician. Gratefully he responded immediately to Stan's needs. Proceeding to Stan's hospital room, this very concerned physician read Stan's chart. He immediately ordered X-rays to be taken of Stan's kidneys. The x-rays were taken as dye was being injected into Stan's veins with an IV. Stan did become violently ill from an allergic reaction to the iodine in the dye. As the very difficult day continued we learned the prognosis was grim. Stan's left kidney was not functioning and was full of pus. It would have to be removed immediately or he would die. His other kidney had a double collecting system. The system would have to be repaired. We were encouraged to understand that Stan would continue to have debilitating infections should he avoid the recommended repairs.

While this was unexpected and disarming news, Stan and I both agreed he would have the required surgeries. Within a few hours the left kidney was removed without any complications. Stan was stitched up and able to leave the hospital several days later. While he wasn't able to stand straight without the stitches pulling, he did his best to stand in the sun and stretch. Giggling, I told him he reminded me of a lizard....one that some mischievous boy had just set loose from a very dark container. With those words, Stan grinned and pulled me close to him. Holding back tears, I returned his hug, feeling relieved that once again we had found answers to prayers.

Chapter Four

UNDERSTANDING GRACE

Driving home Stan explained that he had felt increased anxiety while confined to the hospital. We both concluded he would benefit with a visit to the little mining community of Ouray found nestled within a picturesque mountain valley in southern Colorado. Lying snugly enclosed within a U-shaped valley surrounded by spectacular, soaring mountains on three sides Ouray offers a restorative environment conducive to healing. Our visit would have to be made soon as the golden warmth of the autumn colors would shortly be transformed into a peaceful, snow filled winter. The community would then become almost silent as the last trainload of tourists departed for the season.

The intriguing history of the San Juan Mountains engaged our interest as much as their magnificence. It is reported that the first humans in the San Juan Mountains were the ancestors of the North American Indians who originated in Asia. This group of people were called the basket makers, or the Anasazi—the Ancient Ones. One of many displays in several museums demonstrates that they grew corn and squash while hunting and fishing to supplement their diet. Visiting the museums, one can observe the beauty of their basketry which is famous for its design.

Eventually, other humans arrived on the scene, and settled in with the basket makers. They would become the ancestors of today's Pueblo Indians. These folks made lovely pottery and used bows and arrows as their principal weapons. As they continued to develop building skills, they would learn to create housing that was constructed of adobe. Discussing the possibility of a day drive, we agreed a visit to one of the ruins would also be relaxing. However, we determined that we wouldn't be able to include both the ruins and Ouray into our day trip. A decision was made. Being able to drive into the mountains, enjoying their majesty while perhaps catching a glimpse of a herd of elk was the best option. We would also watch for the fields that would be carpeted with beautiful wildflowers, including a favorite; the Colorado Columbine. Finding such a field would offer a deliciously idle day that would be calming and stimulating at the same time.

Stan and I both understood nature to be an environment in which one can easily contemplate the promises of eternity. Our sojourns into nature had always left a lasting impression of peace and order within our hearts. Beyond our delight with nature, we were always enlightened and stimulated by the sounds, silence and unusual colors found in the natural world. Butterflies would be abundant; they would not hesitate to drop by and share their brilliant colors. Sitting beside a mountain stream listening to the trickle of the water, our senses would expand as we breathed in the fragrant aroma of majestic pine trees. As we discussed possibilities, our souls yearned for what could only be found in nature.

We waited patiently to make the drive into the mountains, allowing a few weeks for Stan's incision to heal. Early one Saturday morning, setting out on our drive, Roger appeared as excited as we were. He loved to hear stories about his great grandfather who had been a miner in his youth. According to family history Grandfather Woods mined in the small community of Silverton, Colorado. A considerable amount of our drive was spent recounting the tales of intrigue that surrounded that mountainous community. Delighting in picturing grandfather riding the narrow gauge train as it worked its way through the narrow passes and along the steep inclines, I encouraged Roger to understand that grandfather was a very prayerful man. We all agreed that the mining folk needed strong faith while battling the winter blizzards and sometimes fatal snow slides they encountered on a regular basis.

As we pulled into a road side stop to take a break, a whisper of a chill breeze reminded us of the blustery winter winds that could drive snow clouds quickly into the mountains. There was a time when those mountains were crawling with prospectors; one had to wonder how they managed to endure the hardships they had been faced with. We were aware that many of the miners and other residents had met with early deaths. Their history is etched on the beautiful gravestones that stand like sentinels in the cemetery overlooking the small community of Silverton. The winter of 1884 had been extremely hard with snow blockading the Denver and Rio Grande Railway for 73 days. 84 people died in snow slides between Silverton and Ouray that year. It was easy to understand and appreciate their need for the little churches one could find in the various mountain communities.

As the mountain communities sprang up, they would bring with them many "firsts". Some of the "firsts" included the first post office, assay office, bank, blacksmith shop, saloon, hotel, grocery and meat market and sawmill. Pictures decorate the walls of most of the buildings in the old mining towns. History speaks expressively through the pictures. People can be observed snowshoeing in every direction. There had been enough gold and silver strikes to engage the interest of a variety of folks. Miners would travel from as far away as Russia to meet their challenges on mountain tops rising to elevations of 12,000 plus feet. Our imaginations were captured by the majesty of it all. Visiting God's creation proved to be restorative and spiritual.

Returning home from our day trip, we realized like the miners and early pioneers, we too could overcome the obstacles we were faced with. Anticipating the birth of our second child, we remained confident that Stan's second kidney surgery would be successful and he would be restored to full health. Within weeks of his first surgery, Stan once again entered the hospital. With his second surgery, his dressings would have to be changed regularly. The hospital was short staffed resulting in me being trained to "wash up" and change his dressings as needed. Finding myself stretched as I continued with my employment as a grocery checker, kept Roger's respiratory therapy going and driving to the hospital to offer Stan support, I remember feeling grateful that I had youth on my side. I also considered the biblical accounts of two sisters, Mary and Martha.

Mary and Martha's story is recorded in several chapters of the New Testament. Apparently the sisters were disciples of Jesus and he had taught them on a variety of occasions. According to the scripture account found in ST John chapter 12 Jesus traveled to Bethany and paid a visit to their home. While in the home, the sisters made supper and Martha served the Savior. Then Mary took a very costly ointment and anointed the feet of Jesus, wiping his feet with her hair. Like Martha, I could be very task oriented. I'm not clear that it happened to Martha but staying task focused might result in me failing to maintain my spiritual focus. Reading and pondering their story, I determined the need for prioritizing. Realizing it would be imperative for me to ask Heavenly Father directly for instruction on how to maintain balance in the midst of very trying times, I did remember the Lord chastising the scribes and Pharisees for their blindness to priorities. Those religious leaders took pride in being exact in what they did. At the same time we are told in Matthew that they "omitted the weightier matters" of justice, mercy and faith. I realized it was wise to remember that some things are clearly more important to the Lord than others. I also learned from a very judicious woman that when we become too task focused we tend to leave out the spiritual aspect of our lives. She emphasized that we then risk becoming "human doings" rather than human beings.

Finding the key to setting priorities and choosing wisely was my challenge. When Heavenly Father gave Moses the Ten Commandments it was made very clear what our first priority has to be. "Thou shalt have no other Gods before me"; meaning my current priority had to be keeping Heavenly Father first in my life. Then my ability to care for my family and their major needs would be greatly enhanced. Everything would fall into its place and I would continue to have the strength and stamina to carry on. This insight felt so relieving to me; I didn't have to have all the answers. I had only to seek the answers from an omnipotent, omniscience, omnibenevolent, Heavenly Father. His divine grace was sufficient for me.

This was my first inkling of a true understanding of grace. Eventually I would come to understand that sustaining grace equips us with strength, courage and wisdom. The gift of grace leads us to a life that is eternally altered. Jesus spoke to grace often because he understood we would have a difficult time comprehending it as it does seem to go against every instinct of humanity. The natural man apparently has an inbuilt resistance to grace. Jesus, while avoiding the use of the word grace, taught us about it through the parables. Consider, if you will, the parable regarding the Pool of Bethesda found in John, chapter 5. In Jerusalem there was a pool of water that was very unusual in that every so often it would bubble for a short period of time. The superstitious people believed that an angel would come into the pool and trouble the water. In addition, they believed that as soon as the bubbling stopped, the first person to step into the pool would then be cured of any disease they were afflicted with. The pool was surrounded by five porches on which large numbers of crippled and sick people remained vigilant, hoping to rush into the bubbling pool and be healed. Among this crowd of people was a man who had been sick for thirty-eight years. He remained by the pool on a thin mattress and because of his disease, he moved very slowly and was unable to enter the pool first. It was his deepest desire to be like other men and be able to stand erect and walk. One Sabbath day, Jesus was visiting the city of Jerusalem and eventually walked near the pool. When Jesus saw the man he asked, "Wilt thou be made whole"? The man replied, "I have no man, when the water is troubled, to put me into the pool; but when I am coming another steppeth down before me". Recognizing the man's faith, Jesus felt great love for him and admonished him to "Rise, take up thy bed and walk". Immediately feeling strength in every limb, the man found he could stretch and flex his muscles, moving his arms and legs. Obediently, he picked up his bed and walked. Because of his faith and through Jesus's healing power the man was completely healed. This parable is an excellent example of grace.

The apostle Paul understood sustaining grace. He understood that with it we can meet every challenge that is thrown at us. We have an all loving God who remains present to our needs, understands our challenges and offers enough grace to support us through every dilemma we are faced with. It is my belief that as we choose to remain teachable, the Lord will instruct us regarding our ability to engage the powers of heaven, thus receiving his grace.

To be clear, as I chose to focus on God's grace I began to realize it is very difficult to comprehend. It is definitely not an easy subject to approach. In my quest for understanding I began to recognize how much easier it is for me to be ungracious rather than gracious. I know what it is to be unforgiving, and withhold love based on being too judgmental. That is the dilemma with grace that C. S. Lewis clarified for me. He quoted St. Augustine, "God gives where he finds empty hands". In other words, a person who has filled their hands with packages will not have room for one that contains the gift of grace. One must leave room for grace to enter their lives which means letting go of real or imagined offenses, hurt feelings and expectations. Letting go means focusing our energy in the present, letting our day flow with grace while realizing eagles soar while flying above the clouds of discontent.

I have come to understand grace is much like dew from heaven. The dewdrops distill upon us and we are nourished spiritually, just as the branch receives nourishment from the vine. Making the choice to focus on grace, I truly came to realize that it takes more than will power or "white knuckling" during challenging times. This realization can be difficult for people like myself who tend to be too self- absorbed. When we finally release ourselves to Heavenly Father, we find that his grace is sufficient. This discovery only comes when we choose to humble ourselves before him, however. One of my favorite hymns is Amazing Grace. As I listen to the healing words of this hymn I am reminded that I want to recognize and experience continued grace in my life. "I once was lost but now I'm found, was blind but now I see" is a consideration for most of us to realize. Considering my blindness makes it possible for me to be open to gifts from the universe as they unexpectedly appear. Then will I recognize and understand joy in the journey has everything to do with grace.

Chapter Five

REFINERS FIRE

Sharing my sought after insights on grace with Stan, we watched and waited for his current surgery to be successful. Success would mean his urethra (the tube responsible for urine leaving the body as it empties from the bladder) would heal. In the meantime he would wear a bag that would collect the urine from his bladder and then be emptied by him. Gratefully there was no need for Stan to remain hospitalized as his body healed. Returning home meant a better night's rest and Stan's return to limited duties at work.

We felt the Lord's love upon us as we continued our daily schedules. Today, realizing a family united in prayer can bring them much spiritual power because of their demonstration of faith, I also understand why we assume the Lord will respond to our petitions. Believing that if a family is praying for what is honorable and right it only stands to reason that the Lord will respond favorably. There is more to the story however. We may be allowed to pass through difficult circumstances, which are very different circumstances from the ones we are seeking, for the welfare of our souls and eternal development.

Realizing each person has a variety of opportunities to pass through the refiner's fire while understanding it is not a comfortable place to be helps a person pay attention to their expectations. As I studied the literal concept of a refiner's fire I learned it involves intense heat and repeated hammering. As Heavenly Father's children the outcome is amazing as it is in the refiner's fire we are purified and prepared to meet him. At the same time, the "hammering" can be very unsettling. Understanding that our God is faithful and will not allow his children to be tried or tempted beyond their capacity to endure is necessary! I came to believe that as we deal with each new challenge, we are blessed with a new kind of power that enables us to rise above our current challenges. That belief still lingers in my soul, whispering words of encouragement at the times I desperately need to hear them.

A few weeks into our vigil with Stan's kidney surgery, on a very cold and overcast morning we set off on our scheduled drive to the clinic in Albuquerque for Roger's check-up. The stars were twinkling in the heavens, the roads were clear and Roger was resting peacefully in the back seat. Absent mindedly, I rubbed my stomach as I felt our baby "kicking". As the sun made its debut from the east, the splendor of the morning was breath taking. I was experiencing such optimism! It felt as though nothing could intrude on our happiness. Suddenly, without warning the car began to swerve. Alarmed, I glanced over at Stan.

"What's happening?" I questioned as he began pulling the car onto the shoulder of the road. "I think we just blew a tire", he responded. "Oh no, how will we change it", I questioned. Stan was quick to reassure me. I had experienced some spotting and had been advised not to do any heavy lifting. And Stan certainly shouldn't do any lifting until his doctor gave him the go ahead. There was no one in sight and no way to call for help. Stan was determined I would not lift anything. He drew a deep breath and went about changing the tire. Later that day, I considered how determined Stan had been to change that tire without complaining and without hesitation. Wrapping my arms around his neck, I expressed my gratitude for his stoic attitude and then I stepped back and gave him a punch in the arm. It wasn't much of a punch, but I needed to let off a little steam as I worried about any damage he might have done to his kidney.

We became apprehensive as the days continued and Stan's system refused to "kick in". Finally, we heard the words that we had been dreading. Stan's urologist was very caring as he explained Stan's need for a third surgery. This news was very disarming. Perhaps we had been naïve, but we expected to hear that Stan's surgery was completely successful. With this news I was again reminded that remaining faithful and prayerful does not mean the door to distress will always close upon our bidding. I remembered a poem I had read on a bookmark. It was written originally by Eliza M. Hickok. Her premise was that God does hear and answer prayer. However in his infinite wisdom, rather than honor our petition, he may actually "send some answer far more blessed". It then occurred to me that timing is everything! Stan could have become ill earlier in the year. We would not have had a specialist available; how amazing it was that the very week we needed him the urologist was there for us. With this insight we chose to remain focused and realize we were blessed with a needed physician, wonderful family and church members and a community of caring people who would remain with us through this difficult time. We also realized the value of understanding the need to connect hope with the will to live. Connecting hope and the will to live directly to the ability of the body to heal is imperative.

Living close to the Navajo reservation had afforded me the opportunity to meet a medicine woman. She was a sister to one of the nurses working in the pediatrics unit at San Juan Hospital. Wearing a lovely purple velvet blouse, a long flowing skirt and amazing turquoise jewelry the day we had our visit, her weathered face appeared rich with wisdom. As I approached her in the open air market where she agreed to meet me I noticed she carried herself with an easy elegance. She was clearly an example of a Navajo woman who had learned to blend her American and Navajo philosophies to carry out her work.

It is my understanding that a Navajo girl experiences a rite of passage where a ritual is performed to ensure a blessed life. This rite of passage is called a kinaalda. At the time this medicine woman's Hozhooja was performed the medicine man announced, "This one has a gift". "Dii bidine eyika adoolwol" he continued. He had just declared his understanding that she would help her people. Thus she began her journey into the healing arts. Being impressed with her wisdom and clarity, I shared my concerns regarding Stan's health. As she explained that some of her patients would benefit with the treatment of herbs, others would benefit with "incantations" and others with modern medicine my regard for her deepened. Declaring that regardless of the chosen path for healing, she emphasized the need to realize each patient carries his own doctor within his soul. She explained the need for us to always seek our "physician" within. As I shared the words of wisdom I had gained from my visit with the medicine woman, Stan acknowledged his part in healing his body. While he definitely didn't look forward to another surgery Stan's level of acceptance afforded him the opportunity to willingly participate in his healing.

Heavenly Father would continue to bless us with an understanding of his grace in the weeks to come. It was hard to imagine how we would financially stay afloat while Stan took more time off for his third surgery. His sick days had been completely wiped out with the previous surgeries. And while we had insurance to cover some of the medical expenses our bank account would continue to be drained. Imagine our relief and gratitude when Stan's co-workers stepped forward to donate their sick days to Stan. Their generosity was stunning! Our relief was immeasurable. Our gratitude was profound. Other tender mercies were made available to us. Checking in with his urologist just previous to his third surgery, we were advised that another surgeon would be assisting our physician. This man had a practice in Albuquerque and he was willing to fly into our little community and assist! Imagine our relief as we received this welcoming news. As he was re-admitted to the hospital, I remember Stan's anxiety level being considerably higher than with the previous surgeries. This made perfect sense to me. It was hard to comprehend all that he had experienced so far and still yet had to face.

I also reflected on the first time I met Stan. We were approaching our junior year in high school and each had decided to join others in a high school tradition. I drove with several girl friends to help whitewash the "F" on the side of the hill which stood for Farmington High School. Stan had arrived with several of his friends. There was no question in my mind how handsome he was when I caught my first glimpse of him. His height was perfect for me. He had broad shoulders and a trim waist which he maintains after 55 years of marriage. His hair was a light brown and his eyes an azure blue. Initially he appeared very intent on accomplishing our goal and then he smiled when he became satisfied with the outcome of our work. His face was transformed with that smile and my heart was captured.

Chapter Six

PATIENCE IN THE PROCESS

"I'll be alright", Stan said in a shaky voice as he emerged from the effects of the anesthesia. Stan was a pale portrait of himself, his hospital gown opening at the side. Through the opening, I noticed the urine output from his single kidney trickled out of his body through a tube he had coming from his incision. Once again it emptied into a bag that he would now watch and empty. In that moment he had my deepest respect. It appeared his first impulse was to ease my concerns. Avoiding eye contact I questioned, "How are you feeling?" If I had been inclined to look into his eyes he would see mine flooded with fear. Though clearly in pain, Stan remained centered. "I will be alright, you know", he calmly reassured me. I did notice however that his smile did not reach his eyes.

In my own mind, I likened his situation to a game of human chess. The urologist had made his move, now it was Stan's turn. With his return to our home, from my heart of hearts I prayed that Stan's body would make a formidable move. We made a commitment to maintain hope and faith through watching for the tender mercies that are afforded each of us every day. Our food would be savored, our sleep appreciated, our family enjoyed. We would embrace the beauty of the sunrise and sunset and read amazing stories of everyday people who met life with courage and valor. Those courageous people helped us find faith we so desperately needed.

My grandmother's maiden name was Israel. Perhaps it is this fact that engaged my interest in the Jews and the sorrows that were thrust upon that group of courageous people. I have come to believe that a visit to Yad Vashem, a memorial for the Holocaust in Jerusalem, would be so impactful. Reading that one can visit a whole library at this memorial and find the names of six million martyrs helped me realize how insignificant our challenges were. Not only does the library list their names it also gives details describing where they lived, where they were born, and other details of their lives. Their stories demonstrate that they existed and their lives mattered. While a visit to their memorial wasn't possible being a witness to their sacrifices through reading and studying was very much possible.

In considering the Holocaust, I want to focus on the history of a woman found in the book, "The Hiding Place". While many people are aware of Corrie's experiences, there is value in refreshing our memories. Corrie's story serves to remind us that there are people who are very capable of committing atrocious crimes against humanity. And in the midst of those conflicts there are people who carefully and quietly fight against the evil. This story is one of amazing faith.

Corrie ten Boom and her family became leaders in the Dutch Underground during the Nazi invasion and occupation of Holland. This incredibly courageous Christian family hid Jewish people in their home in a specially built room and aided in their escape from the Nazis. Eventually, because of the choices they made to rescue the Jews, Corrie and her family were arrested and placed in barracks within the dreaded concentration camps. Corrie related that she barely escaped death during her incarceration. She described a daily existence of brutality at the camp called Ravensbruck. Corrie's beloved sister Betsie did meet death in the dreaded barracks of Ravensbruck. Corrie had concealed a bible while incarcerated and shared it with her fellow prisoners. The words from the bible had served as anchors for herself and other women.

Eventually Corrie was released and returned to her old home. Remembering days spent with family and friends within its walls, she began to understand what the future would look like. She realized that people must be told what she and her sister Betsie had experienced and learned. The most important message she would share was her understanding that joy runs deeper than despair.

Embracing this insight, Stan and I again concluded it would be judicious for us to embrace our joys and continue to live with patience in our hearts while avoiding any inkling of despair. We also came to realize that just because we wanted to live patiently didn't mean we had to cease being hopeful. This is when I began to realize the importance of practicing "patience in the process". Obviously we were in the process of going through the refiner's fire and learning to trust in the Lord and his timing. Once again, this understanding really resonated with me and I became even more determined to live in the moment. I was also truly beginning to understand that our ability to practice patience evolves as we develop inner peace. I have learned that peace comes as we push through the problems of this life rather than folding in despair and self-pity.

It was also helpful to realize that patience can be learned. Realizing that patience is one of those heavenly virtues that some people are gifted with, I knew that I was not one of those people. Instead of practicing patience I would rather wring my hands in despair and stamp my foot in a petulant fashion. Gratefully I had family and friends who would not allow my show of impatience to linger. Oliver Goldsmith stated, "The greatest object in the universe is a good man (it was obvious to me he was also referring to women) struggling with adversity; yet there is still a greater, which is the good man who comes to relieve it." About the same time I was beginning to comprehend how many really good people we had in our lives, I received a note from my uncle. In it he stated, "No man is an island unto himself". Having experienced a variety of adversities over the years, we have also experienced so many gracious people who were willing to live outside themselves in love and service to others.

Recalling numerous examples of people who lived in other times in a variety of places, their trials and tribulations speaks volumes regarding their faithfulness in the face of adversity. Isaiah must have realized he would face much adversity should he accept the ministry that was extended to him in Isaiah, chapter six. In this chapter, Isaiah actually sees the Lord sitting upon a throne and then has his sins forgiven. Just before his sins are forgiven I picture him as wringing his hands in anguish (that's what I would be doing), speaking the words, "Woe is me! For I am undone; because I am a man of unclean lips, and I dwell in the midst of a people of unclean lips; for mine eye have seen the King, the Lord of hosts." I don't believe Isaiah's awareness of his unworthiness to be in the presence of Heavenly Father is a unique experience. And after coming under the influence of the Holy Ghost he was able to volunteer to serve saying, "Here am I, send me". Consider Daniel who was one of the choice sons of Israel. After being taken captive and taken into a wicked nation he was raised up for a wicked kings' own purposes. Because he and other captives were seen as the better of the lot they were fed from the kings table. While this was supposed to be a gift from the king, it was seen as a real trial for Daniel. Meat and the wine that was served were against Daniel's standards and he risked his life when he found a guard who agreed to feed him grains. As he took his stand against the adversity he was facing, Daniel was blessed with physical well- being and hidden treasures of wisdom.

Studying the words of our Savior, I know that his life is our ultimate example of patience as he faced the harshest adversity. While in the Garden of Gethsemane he asked, if possible, for the cup of his suffering be taken from him. "Nevertheless", he said, "not as I will, but as thou wilt" (Matthew 26:39). The realization that we'll all be required to wait for things in our lives was becoming ever clearer to me. It also became clear to me that we'll never have to be alone in our waiting. Jesus Christ will provide us with comfort and reassurance as we face our trials and tribulations. He speaks volumes to our hearts through the blue skies and quiet green grass. He whispers his love in leaves on the trees, while birds sit among those trees whistling cheerful songs to us. His love clothes us with warm sunshine in our days and spills moonlight upon our faces at night. As our minds remain active and engaged, we will be delighted with his boundless love. And so, Stan and I waited and watched realizing that in our hopeful state of being we would also be drawing closer to our Savior.

Stan did have a bit of a male stubborn streak and was finding it very difficult to let go and allow for a support system of people to help us. The birth of our second child was fast approaching and we also had that experience to look forward to. Focusing on Romans 8:28 and realizing that Heavenly Father will make all things in our lives work together for our good was valuable. Remembering a favored prose I had read was also very useful. The periodicals it came from had been entitled "The Humbler Poets" and had been published around 1870 to 1885. The prose is entitled "The Dawn". The words that stood out in my mind rang true for us, "Pain cannot affect us always, brighter days will soon be here; Sorrow may oppress us often, yet a happier time is near. All along our earthly journey this reflection lights the way; Nature's darkest hour is always just before the day".

The six long weeks of waiting and watching for a miracle had felt endless. Can you imagine our relief and delight the day Stan's ureter made its remarkable move? Our happy dance was quite silly and not worthy of much mention. Realizing our darkest hour had passed, I quickly prepared his favorite meal of crispy fried chicken, fried okra, hot dinner rolls drenched in butter, mashed potatoes with cream gravy and chocolate meringue pie. We didn't yet have to worry about high cholesterol!

Through this time of waiting and watching we came to realize the value of making peace with our bodies, even as they appear to be falling short of expectations. Somewhere in his life, Stan had become hardwired for work. Life and work for him were one and the same. Not only was he eager to return to his employment, he was eager to return to his "yard" work. I have a brother who has commented, "You can always tell which house is Stan's by the immaculate lawn". Once again we were able to relax and enjoy our family and daily living.

Our son Dennis was born within that year. His birth was normal and I felt immediate relief when I "tasted" him and found no evidence of salt. Roger had waited six years for a sibling and he was elated with the birth of his baby brother. Within a few hours of bringing Dennis home from the hospital I heard voices at our front door. Roger had raced around our neighborhood collecting his friends. His excitement had touched their young souls and they were all eager to meet the new arrival.

While Roger had been blessed with many material gifts from thoughtful family members and friends, he recognized the value of an eternal family. Considering his one unique quality I would choose the word faithful. Roger's personality was grounded in his faithful understanding and love for the Savior. C.S. Lewis was a novelist, poet, academic, literary critic, lay theologian, and Christian apologist. In his faithful loyalty to our Savior, he taught that it is when we turn to Christ, when we give ourselves up to his personality, that we first begin to have a real personality of our own. Roger had his own personality; he loved powerfully and unconditionally.

With another son to enjoy, we resumed our lives, becoming involved in favored activities. While the mountains continued to call to us, we also enjoyed camping and fishing at Navajo Dam. This dam was built as part of the Colorado River Storage Project. It is located on the meandering San Juan River in northeastern New Mexico about 35 miles east of Farmington. Home to deer and coyote it also has a population of pole cats who enjoy visiting the camp grounds located just below the dam.

One particular evening I was relaxing in front of a mellow camp fire, enjoying my current book. I had already put the boys to bed in our pick-up camper. As I drifted between sleeping and reading, my senses alerted me that something was amiss. Cautiously I appraised the campground with a quick glance. Imagine my alarm when I discovered a skunk, alias "pole cat", sniffing around the foot of the steps leading into our camper. I had left the door propped open in order to listen for the boys. Freezing, I realized I didn't want to startle that little varmint. Any sudden movement might send it scooting right up those steps and into the camper. Startling it in any way could also mean it would give off the most awful, foul smell. I'm quite clear a skunk's "chemical defense" is very effective in keeping them safe. My heart was pounding so hard, I was afraid it would give me away. It seemed like it took forever for that "little stinker" to make up its mind. As calmly and deliberately as it had walked into our campground, our unwelcome visitor finally turned and walked away. Needless to say, I created a plan for keeping watch on the sleeping boys while keeping the camper door closed! When Stan returned to our campground with his fishing pole and catch in hand he was a bit too amused with my story of our visitor.

Considering our joy in having Roger and Dennis in our lives, I am reminded of the words spoken by the poet Kahlil Gibran. He stated, "You are the bows from which your children are sent forth". His words reminded me that our Heavenly Father allows us stewardship over our children so that we might prepare to "launch" them into the world, armed with living skills and spiritual insights we have helped them develop. He has also blessed each of us with talents that we are able to strengthen as we choose. Our son Dennis came prepared to share his wisdom through humor. He would sometimes stop me in my tracks with his gift of humor. Eventually I came to realize through his example that "angels can fly because they take life lightly". Not that I have fully developed this skill. I have found it very useful to remember that a daily dose of humor can relieve many a heavy load.

Being an avid cub scout, Roger's competitive side became apparent when he made his first pine wood derby car. He was so excited when he was awarded a ribbon for that car. I was his den mother and had a yellow Volkswagen "bug" as my only mode of transportation. Each week following our den meeting, we would load up some of the boys to drive them home. You couldn't begin to hear yourself think as each boy had a new joke to tell or a story regarding their day at school.

These young boys delighted in learning to offer little acts of service to others. As they earned their badges, we focused on leaders of our nation and the contributions they made to mankind. Imagine their dismay to learn that George Washington with his little hatchet had not cut down the cherry tree! According to author James Thomas Fletcher the cherry tree story was a fabrication. Flexner emphasized that Washington perfected himself gradually through the exercise of his will and skill. Flexner believed Washington to be one of the noblest and greatest men who ever lived, describing him as more than a military leader. He described him as the eagle, the standard, the flag, and the living symbol of the cause for liberty. In studying Washington and his drive to pursue liberty, I invited the cub scouts to consider President Washington's concerns regarding the youth of his time. His primary concern was that they were in danger of becoming "indolent and helpless" as they were so well taken care of. In Washington's time the youth were given a horse with a servant to attend them as soon as they could ride. The young cub scouts appeared to comprehend the love and respect that Washington gained from his fellowmen because of his commitment to doing his part. Washington's words "The confidence and affections of his fellow citizens is the most valuable and agreeable reward a citizen can achieve" appeared to ring true to their young ears. They seemed to realize that no peace or freedom can come to this world so long as men live only for themselves.

We continued in our home to stress the need for understanding and comprehending the true meaning and purpose of prayer. In an article on prayer Chauncey C. Riddle declared that one fundamental distinction between the saint and what the scriptures call the "natural man" is their use of prayer. He related that the natural man may say prayers but it is not a spiritual experience for him. He is only reacting to his physical environment as he has been instructed or as he thinks prudent. Riddle stated "praying, as distinct from merely saying prayers, has a spiritual dimension. The transformation from a natural man to a saint is marked by the ability to recognize and to respond to the spiritual environment".

I have also found it invaluable to realize that while communicating with my Father in Heaven that it is imperative to maintain faith in Jesus Christ. We end our prayers, "in the name of Jesus Christ" because we're asking for the grace of Jesus Christ to intervene on our behalf.

Chapter Seven

I CAN DO ALL THINGS THROUGH CHRIST

Our son Dennis was three years old when I began to feel "stirrings" in my spirit. Quite possibly, only a woman can understand the feeling that I'm attempting to describe. I had always believed that we would have a baby girl and her name would be Amanda. Stan and I both had continued to be delighted and grateful our son Dennis was thriving. He exhibited no signs of the dreaded Cystic Fibrosis. As the days continued from fall into winter, my promptings grew stronger. Approaching Stan one evening I stated, "we have a baby daughter waiting to join our family. I know her name; she will be called Amanda". Stan's expression gave his thoughts away. He apparently was having similar feelings and had hesitated to share them. Now his relief was apparent. He agreed we would benefit as we turned to Heavenly Father in prayer, seeking to know his will regarding the addition of another child to our home. It has been our experience that as we begin our day in prayer and then continue with our day while walking with that prayer in our heart, we will be blessed in our efforts. We also realized the need to avoid becoming fanatical in our prayers understanding that the adversary is neither moderate nor temperate. In time, we felt a divine calming influence and knew what course to pursue. We would experience another pregnancy. It is of value to bear in mind that we make the effort, we do not control the outcome. And while making that effort, realize that as the problems continue, remaining divinely centered one will maintain their faith and optimism.

Several days previous to our baby's birth, we had to admit Roger to the hospital in Farmington. Once again he was struggling to live. As the evening of October 11th drew to a close and Roger was ready for sleep, I explained to him and Stan that I needed a few hours of rest. I suspected the baby would soon make her appearance. While it was hard for me to leave Roger, I knew he understood my plans. Departing the hospital and arriving at the home of my in-laws a short time later, I explained my course of action to them as I collected our son Dennis. They lived two minutes from our home and were very supportive of my needs. Arriving home, I tucked Dennis into his bed, drew a shower and began to sort out what was next. Finally, I lay down for a "nap". The few hours of rest were refreshing; little did I know it would be several days before I would again have that opportunity.

It was around midnight when I understood I needed to return to the hospital. My labor pains were much stronger and closer together. While I had expected more time to rest, this was not to be the case. Dropping Dennis off at my in-laws, I drove back to the hospital. Parking close to the window of Roger's room, I very carefully stepped down from the seat of the truck. Tapping on the screen of his window, I awoke Stan and asked him to meet me back in the emergency room. It was the only unlocked entrance into the hospital this time of night.

Suddenly realizing my contractions were increasing, I also understood I couldn't pull myself back up into the truck. As I cautiously began walking toward the back of the hospital, I noticed a side door was standing open, propped by a chair. What a relief! This door led directly into the hallway that would connect with the delivery room. Feeling hopeful, I walked through the door right into the arms of a very caring nurse. She helped me into a wheel chair and quickly whisked me off to the delivery room.

Stan, in the meantime, had rushed to the emergency room only to discover I hadn't yet arrived! Feeling alarmed, he and a security guard shot out into the parking lot to search for me. Experiencing a bit of a frantic panic, it would take a few moments for them to realize I wasn't outside. As quickly as he had searched the parking lot Stan joined me. Recovering from his moment of bewilderment (we did have a bit of a chuckle over the few minutes of craziness when he hadn't been able to find me), we both concluded he should return to Roger and keep him informed of my progress.

It was daybreak when our little daughter was born. Her delivery was difficult and I sensed something was very wrong. Immediately upon her birth, the physician placed her on my stomach and wrote a note to the nurse. Then Cynthia was whisked away by another nurse. Feeling considerable alarm, I began seeking information from the physician. He explained that our baby girl was in obvious distress. With her birth it was clear that she had Cystic Fibrosis. The thick mucus that creates lung problems can also create severe digestive problems. Cynthia had an intestinal blockage called meconium ileus. Her very swollen stomach was what had made her delivery so difficult. She would have to have surgery as soon as possible. We had not prepared ourselves for this scenario as we did not realize the possibility of problems at birth.

Carefully I made my way to Roger's room. While her delivery had been very difficult and my body needed to heal, I felt compelled to speak with Roger and explain Cynthia's circumstances to him. Upon learning of her distress and pending surgery, Roger explained he wanted one year with his baby sister. Asking that we pray together, Stan and I were quick to agree. Thanking Heavenly Father for the gift of these precious spirits in our lives, I submitted Roger's request for a year with his baby sister. Realizing how stacked the odds were against either of our children leaving the hospital, I also realized that Heavenly Father is a God of miracles.

Returning to the surgical waiting area, I continued my vigilance. Stan remained with Roger to assist in his respiratory therapy. It would be several hours before the surgeon would appear with news of Cynthia. He appeared grim as he approached me and my heart sank. Sadly he shook his head as he stated, "She is just too diseased to live". Asking where I could find her, he stated she would be in an incubator in the newborn nursery. I quickly described my need to attend to her. Explaining that I couldn't be with Roger and then return to the newborn nursery because of the risk involved, I listened carefully and then requested further information from him. The surgeon was gentle as he shared that the risk of carrying bacteria from Roger to Cynthia was considerable. Puzzled, I asked how our pediatrician would be able to attend to the needs of both children. The surgeon stated that our pediatrician would scrub up before entering their rooms. Apparently there was a room for this process to take place in.

Advising the surgeon that I understood the need to scrub up, I also advised him that both of my children required attention from their mother. Requesting his support in this need, the surgeon agreed that I could be taught to "scrub up" and then be able to attend to both children. Relief washed over me as I heard his words.

Because Cynthia was in an incubator and couldn't be held, I was able to soothe her by reaching in and patting her tiny back while speaking softly to her. The nurses told me my soothing her was very helpful as they didn't want her crying and thrashing about, risking the loss of her IV. They placed a rocking chair beside her incubator so that I could sit and rest in it when she was resting. The nursing staff were so amazing in their capacity to offer empathy and support.

Moving between both children, I had the opportunity to reflect on many thoughts. Remembering a poem by Khalil Gibran called "On Death", I realized these were some of the hardest moments of my life because of my fear of death. Should I choose to follow Gibran's admonition I would come to realize that we find answers to death through living in "the heart of life".

Slowly, my perception began to shift. Rather than fear the loss of one or several of my beloved children, it would behoove me to relish our minutes together. Cynthia had a second surgery when she was five days old. As I continued my vigilance with her, I sometimes felt that if I moved my head quickly enough I would be able to observe the presence of angels watching over her. It gradually occurred to me that a very important decision was being made. Realizing that angels represent God and serve as they are assigned among mortals, I have not found any evidence of a guardian angel being assigned indefinitely to each individual. I do believe they are present to serve a guardian role to warn, protect and strengthen as God sees fit. I want to emphasize my realization that we were experiencing a very sacred time in our life and I feel cautious in my sharing. I would never want these heavenly moments treated lightly. Understanding that angels in our midst confirms God's existence makes the difficulties of this journey more manageable and offers hope in times of distress.

Early one morning, I was asleep on a couch that was in a small waiting room close to the newborn nursery. I awoke with a start to discover our pediatrician standing over me. He informed me that he needed to do a blood transfusion directly from me into Cynthia. Quickly scrubbing up we entered the nursery together. I remember everything being so quiet and still. I wanted so much for her and her brother Roger to have some time together and for each of us to get to know her. At the same time, she had already experienced so much physical pain. Was I asking for too much? After our pediatrician completed the transfusion he left me alone with our baby girl. He related to me that if she lived to the break of dawn, she would have a chance of surviving. Shadows wrapped her room in darkness, as I stood beside her incubator. As dawn neared, I felt an intense longing. I realized that with daybreak, the clouds would be bathed in a golden light and I experienced such powerful hope filling my soul! As a family we had prayed for a miracle. Now realizing we were in the presence of angels I knew I had to "be still" within my soul and have patience in this sacred process. As I reached into the incubator and nestled her tiny fist, Cynthia grasped my finger and held on so tightly. She seemed to want to encourage me!! In turn I reflected again on the poem by Eliza M. Hickok, feeling encouraged to realize that God does answer prayer and sometimes we will receive "some answer far more blessed". Finally I received a confirmation within my soul; our little baby girl would live!

As we waited and watched over our baby daughter, a miracle was afforded us. Roger's condition had improved enough that he was allowed to return to our home. With this miracle I was reminded that nothing is impossible with the Lord. Reflecting on the story of Abraham and Sarah, I again realized that the Lord does his best work in circumstances that are impossible. When the Lord promised that Abraham and Sarah would have a child in their old age, Sarah questioned the possibility of such a happening. She was admonished, "Is there anything too hard for the Lord?" And then there is the account found in Luke, chapter one. Elisabeth had been barren all her life when she was promised a son in her old age. She was reminded, "For with God nothing shall be impossible". I have come to realize that the Lord does his best work in circumstances that are impossible or at least near to it! I'm also aware that we cannot serve two masters at the same time. Doubt and fear cannot reside in the mind of man (woman) at the same time as faith. Each of us are given opportunities to notice when our fears are over-whelming our ability to experience faith. The scriptures are replete with stories of people who learned this valuable lesson.

For example, one of my favorite paintings that hangs in my home is of Jesus approaching his disciples on the surface of the sea. We find the account of this painting in Matthew 14. Jesus had encouraged his disciples to board a ship and "go before him unto the other side" while he sent the multitudes he had fed away. After going up into the mountain to pray alone, Jesus went to the disciples, walking on the waves that had become turbulent from the rising wind. When the disciples saw him, they cried out in fear believing him to be a spirit. He responded by encouraging them to realize who he was and to be of good cheer. Peter responded, "Lord, if it be thou, bid me come unto thee on the water". As Jesus invited him, Peter stepped out of the boat. Imagine Peter's feelings when he began to put all of his weight onto his foot and started to step into the Sea of Galilee. Suddenly he found himself walking on water! Then the adversary made his appearance. As the wind stirred up, the waves swelled higher and Peter, in fear, began to doubt. As he filled with fear, Peter began sinking into that dark, turbulent water. Then Jesus reached out to save him, saying "O thou of little faith, wherefore didst thou doubt?" It is my experience that the greatest challenge is to really believe with all our hearts that the Lord will be involved in the details of our lives as we invite him in. And we also will benefit as we recognize how much the adversary would use fear to weaken our faith.

As I continued my vigilance over our infant daughter, I remained faithful. It would be a few days later when Stan and I were again approached by Cynthia's surgeon. He advised us that Cynthia would require a third surgery. As he shared this news, I questioned him about his belief in prayer. He advised me that he was a prayerful man of faith and if Cynthia were to have any possibility of life, she would need this surgery. We could not deny her this opportunity for life. Returning to her incubator I stood gazing down at our beautiful, blue-eyed angelic baby and thanked our Heavenly Father for her sweet spirit which was gracing our lives with her presence. Once again Cynthia was taken into surgery. Seeking the Lord in prayer we asked that we might continue to be strengthened in the days to come. Almost immediately I felt myself suffused with new strength. It was as if the blessing of a blanket of energy was placed over my body. Finally her surgeon approached us and told us the surgery was complete; now we would wait and watch. Realizing I had to attend to our home and our other children while Stan returned to work, I began a routine that would last another week. Spending time with Cynthia was imperative and when I would have to leave her I remained confident that she was being watched over by angels.

Chapter Eight

FORWARD IN FAITH

It is incredibly valuable to understand that happiness does not necessarily require the absence of adversity. It would be unrealistic to believe that one can go through life without facing trials and tribulations. Studying the oppositions that Job faced allows one to realize that facing the opposition is part of the journey. If we allow ourselves to ask "why me" there is the possibility that our vision will become clouded with our questioning. Our stamina can become quickly depleted as we enter the realm of self-pity. Our hearts can become hardened. We cannot nurture the best part of us while living in this state of woe. Over the course of many years and a number of adversities I have come to realize it is wise to remember we have a divine birthright. Recognizing our responsibility and obligation to cultivate the very best qualities within us is imperative. When Helen Keller was asked what could be worse than being blind, she responded, "Having eyes to see…and no vision". It would be invaluable for Stan and me to move forward in faith regarding our two very seriously ill children. Roger's prayerful request for a year with his sister was not an impossibility. To remain open to his petition meant we must cast out all doubt and fear and maintain the faith Roger was demonstrating.

I will never forget the relief and gratitude I experienced when our pediatrician approached me with amazing news. Cynthia would be released to our care within several hours. Immediately calling Stan, he related he would be able to take off work a few hours early in order to help me drive her home. A nurse who worked in the newborn nursery and who had been so supportive through our ordeal approached me with an amazing gift. She had been collecting coupons from the boxes of disposable diapers she used each day. She offered me enough coupons to keep us in disposable diapers for over six months! This would be helpful as Cynthia would continue to have considerable diarrhea. The Lord's hand was evident in all that was taking place this most glorious day.

Pink roses sent from my sister Nancy were delivered to our home minutes after we had arrived there with our precious little one. Cynthia had appeared "plump" while in the incubator. Our pediatrician warned us to be prepared for her appearance to be altered once her IV was removed. Placing her in a comfy baby gown for our drive home, his words rang true as we were very startled by her look of emaciation. Arriving home we laid her beside one of the lovely roses for a baby picture and began to imagine her as our "little pink rose". Realizing that roses refresh the soul and bring feelings of peace, we were grateful for the gift of flowers from my sister and especially the gift of our little daughter. Roger and Dennis stood by eagerly awaiting their turn to hold their baby sister. Dennis was very tender when I placed Cynthia into his arms. He was sitting on the sofa and as he took her from me his expression was one of thoughtful consideration. I quickly whispered to him, "Hey, she is going to be okay". Looking up at me I could see a tear streaming down his cheek. Realizing he must be filled with so many questions, I wanted to give him permission to address each one, in his own time frame. As Cynthia settled comfortably into his shoulder, Dennis let out an audible sigh. He appeared so relieved. After a few minutes, Cynthia began to stir in his arms and Dennis asked Roger if he was ready to hold her.

Roger was beaming as we presented him with his baby sister. He was now eleven years old and barely weighed 40 pounds. In the previous year he had begun to use oxygen on a daily basis. We had a portable canister that we pushed around on a cart when we were away from home. While at home, we used a very long piece of tubing which allowed Roger to move freely from room to room. Being extra careful to avoid entangling the oxygen tubing I carefully placed Cynthia on Roger's shoulder. He softly began singing her a lullaby. Our baby girl appeared to be soothed by the presence of her brothers. Paying close attention to our children during these moments I reminded myself how much a chronic illness can affect family dynamics. Realizing I would be caught up in the emotional and physical care of both Roger and Cynthia I quickly resolved to make every effort to recognize the needs of Dennis and not allow his needs to fall by the wayside. Gratefully several of my friends also recognized the need to support Dennis and were very helpful in considering his needs. One of them appeared at our door one day to plan a birthday party for Dennis. She had on a clown suit and was eager to make his birthday a very special time.

My mind is flooded with examples of people and their generosity during this difficult time. Being a patriot in every sense of the word, Roger had grandfathers and uncles who had served in the military and he appreciated their service. His grandmother was very creative and concluded Roger would enjoy having his portable oxygen canister painted red, white and blue. His Uncle Mike who had served overseas was happy to paint Roger's bedroom red, white and blue! Our neighbors were school teachers. Because Roger was too ill and too vulnerable to childhood colds and flu, this couple agreed to home school him. One project he really enjoyed doing with them involved putting together and launching a rocket. It would be painted red, white and blue.

We were once again faced with serious medical expenses. Roger's major medical insurance had been depleted. And Cynthia's health insurance didn't kick in until she was six weeks old. We were barely avoiding the edge of bankruptcy. Our children required continuing care around the clock. It wouldn't be feasible for me to return to work. Can you imagine our relief when a very large truck pulled up in front of our home early one morning? The cheerful driver strode to our door and asked where we wanted the tank of oxygen he was delivering to be placed. It was a huge tank!! He assured us it would always be kept full and we would never have to be concerned about it running low. At the time I remember thinking we were surrounded by angels in our own community of Farmington! Stan quickly pointed the man to a spot just beneath Roger's window. The tank would be placed there and the tubing would go directly into Roger's room. Roger had yearned for a dog. We couldn't possibly afford to buy him a dog that would have a non-allergic fur. He was so very happy when a friend called to offer him an adorable silver poodle. Roger's new little companion quickly became very protective of him and when anyone drew too close to his oxygen tubing she would let out a warning growl. Her sense of the value of the oxygen and tubing to Roger was uncanny.

I have heard an analogy of spiritual growth related to that of climbing a mountain. I also appreciate the idea that sometimes we need to take a break and rest as we climb. With Roger's climb, he didn't appear to take many breaks. In spite of struggling for air and becoming weaker with each passing day, Roger continued toward spiritual graduate school. One evening I fell asleep beside him; not intending to do so. We kept his room very cool as his body remained far too warm for him to be comfortable. I had curled up into a ball, feeling quite chilly. I awoke to find Roger struggling to cover me up. As far as he was able Roger took care of those around him.

Having been essentially confined now to our home except for trips out to the doctor and laboratory for blood work, we searched for ways to bring the world to him. We had a CB radio in our pick-up and it occurred to Stan that we should put one in Roger's room. This was a time before cell phones were even a ghost of an idea. Using his CB one day to check in with me as I was running errands, a local businessman interrupted our conversation to inform us we were not allowed to use this particular channel. He stated it needed to remain open for any business person who had to contact someone. We became very quiet and chose not to change channels until we further investigated what channel to use. I'm not clear how the situation shifted but Roger was delighted a few hours later when he heard a man's voice stating, "Roger Dodger, are you there?" Roger came back with a reassuring, "that's a 10-4". The group of businessmen had learned of his being home bound. He was delighted when they asked him to be their "dispatcher". They would call Roger on the CB radio and make a request; perhaps someone was running late for a meeting, needed more material brought to a work site, wanted lunch delivered, etc. Roger would then use our "landline" to assist them in getting their needs met. This group of people had created a thoughtful way for Roger to continue experiencing meaning and purpose in his life.

Concluding Roger would enjoy a train with a village, Stan set up a sheet of 4x8 plywood on sawhorses in his bedroom. We purchased a model train along with a small village for the train to pass through. The bicentennial 1776 locomotive really impressed Roger. Just as we arrived at the perfect set-up a new idea would evolve and the village with scenic mountains in the background became quite impressive!

I would be remiss were I not to mention Roger's love of music. He especially enjoyed the melody and words of the hymn "You're Not Alone". This music rang of truth and hope for him and for us. One of his favorite Christmas hymns had evolved from the poetry of Placide Cappeau de Roquemaure, a poet from the countryside of France. Cappeau was the commissionaire of wines in a small French town. In 1847, his parish priest approached him with a request that might have been startling to the young man as it is written that he was known more for his poetry than his church attendance. The priest asked the wine commissionaire to write a poem for Christmas mass. Realizing the words must focus on scripture, Christmas, and be religious, Cappeau was inspired to write words that testified of the Savior's birth. After completing his work, Cappeau approached a friend who was a master musician. His friend was of Jewish ancestry and didn't celebrate Christmas. Yet together, these men produced music that brings Christmas to life. Each time I have the opportunity to hear or join in the singing of "O Holy Night", I reflect on the joy this Christmas melody brought to Roger's heart. When he felt well enough Roger would choose to stand propped against the record player that was encased in a sturdy cabinet and play his music. While he also enjoyed some country western singers, Elvis Presley would remain his favorite vocalist.

We did take our children out for occasional drives by using Roger's portable oxygen canister. Enjoying a chance to be outside in the beauty of nature was a real treat. During one of our outings we discovered an eagle's nest resting atop a very tall tree just across the river from where we parked. We were all fascinated with the magnificence of the birds. Stan explained to us that the eagles build their nest by taking long, sharp sticks and weaving them together so they all aim straight up through the nest. We felt uncomfortable just hearing Stan's description of the process and asked why the nest had to be built in this fashion. Stan continued with his explanation, stating the mother eagle does "pad" the nest with feathers, grass and leaves. After she finishes padding the nest the mother eagle then lays her eggs in it. He then informed us that usually only one or two baby eaglets would survive. Stating they break out of their eggs with their beaks and find the comfortable nest their mom has prepared for them he continued to explain the eaglets pretty much have it made as long as their mom returns each day with food. As the eaglets continue to grow, their mother realizes it's time for them to leave home. Imagine our shock to learn how they "get booted out"! The mother eagle now begins pulling the comfortable padding from the nest and the little ones grow increasingly uncomfortable as they find themselves resting on sharp objects. I'm not clear how much time lapses (and neither was Stan) when the mother concludes it's time for her little munchkins to soar out into the world on their own. Somehow she communicates to them that they need to climb upon her wings. I can imagine they are quite delighted to be settled into their mom's feathers. Roger also thought this was great. However, Stan explained the "rest of the story". The mother dives out of her nest, flies out over the countryside and begins to soar upward. Suddenly she turns upside down and begins shaking those babies off her wings! I'm not sure whether it was my eyes or Roger's eyes that were the widest with concern as Stan explained this to us. Gratefully, mamma eagle comes through and catches her babies before they crash to the earth! Then she continues the "lesson" all over again. Hopefully these are really bright babies and they catch on quickly! Once they do "learn their lesson", they fly away and are launched permanently into the world. We were never fortunate enough to see the launching of the babies. And we were once again very impressed with "mother nature".

Chapter Nine

GOODNESS AND MERCY

The darkness was finally began to vanish, daybreak was making a magnificent and welcome appearance when I heard Roger softly call out to me. While we had given him a bell to ring whenever he had need of us, Roger continued to hesitate using it, not wanting to awaken his siblings. I quickly threw on my bathrobe and went into him, hoping he had found a few hours of rest. It had been months since he had been able to lay back on a pillow and sleep. Now he slept with his pillows tucked up in front of him and he lay propped in an upright position onto them. He was attempting to clear his oxygen cannula, as his nose had begun bleeding. These were the moments that were the most difficult for him. His oxygen was a double edged sword; while he was dependent on it, it would still cause him difficulty as it would dry out his nasal passage and cause the nose bleeds. We always hoped they would subside quickly. Gratefully this nosebleed proved to be short lived.

Psalm 23 was Roger's favorite Psalm. As he lay forward upon his stacked pillows, Roger began quoting words of peace and solace. He appeared to realize like Isaiah from the Old Testament that we are all in need of a shepherd. And in great times of tribulation, we must turn to our Savior for tranquility and seek His "still waters". In those still waters we will find goodness and mercy. How priceless were those minutes spent with this "little man" who was truly a spiritual giant. Returning to my room to quickly shower and dress, I planned my day.

Roger now required respiratory and physical therapy four times a day. His "treatments" could take up to an hour to complete depending on how much coughing and choking he would have to recover from. Our little Cynthia would also require her treatments. They were not as intensive and would not require as much time however. I suddenly felt incredible gratitude for the support that would soon be appearing at our day. I knew my younger sister Mary would arrive with her cheerful personality to take Cynthia out for a "stroller ride". The baby stroller was a gift from a stranger who must have realized how convenient one would be in our lives with our little infant. In the meantime a benevolent friend would drop her children off at school and show up at our home to help with laundry and dishes. Another would come prepared to do shopping or other errands. I truly was not alone in meeting the challenges the day would bring.

"Will you be able to drive Roger to the cemetery today", Stan inquired as he gave me a quick hug on the way out the door. Roger had been giving thought to his burial for weeks now. He had asked that we put the words of his favorite primary song on his marker. "I am a Child of God", rang so true for him that he wanted his marker to remind others who they are as well. Having visited the cemeteries in old mining towns as well as the local one, Roger had begun the process of accepting his mortality. He had great grandparents, great aunts and uncles, and other distant relatives buried in our local cemetery. When we would visit it Roger would join us in straightening flowers on graves, standing up floral displays and making sure flags remained in an upright position. He continued to enjoy "reading stories" of people's lives found on the markers. Unique people whose stories would not be found in history books. Today the memorial grounds would be mostly empty except for the occasional squirrel scampering ahead of our footsteps.

Being thoughtful in his planning he had also written down what he wanted done with some of his personal items. Many folks might believe these actions to be a bit morbid. For some time now, Roger had been very limited in what he could do physically. Taking control of his final days on earth gave Roger a sense of empowerment. He was also at peace with himself. As a very young boy, barely 11 years of age, Roger had learned to live "in grace", as much of the time as possible. This meant that he had an inner harmony that was essentially spiritual. There was a freshness about Roger that was like a spring morning. My heart ached as I realized how much I would miss his very calming presence.

I also realized that for much of the early twentieth century speaking openly about death was frowned upon as many people believed it to be in poor taste. Gratefully, the psychiatrist Elisabeth Kubler-Ross had begun "dragging death out of darkness". Her book on "Children and Death" has been a close companion of mine, helping me realize how many brave young souls have returned to their Heavenly Father's home. This book is based on Kubler-Ross's decade of working with dying children and brings hope and courage to anyone with a terminally ill child. In addition realizing that death is as indispensable to our eternal development as mortal life itself, embracing the plan of salvation bolstered my faith and brought me solace.

Placing Roger and his portable oxygen tank in our car, I asked him what song he would like to sing. While neither of us could carry a tune, we would drive with the windows rolled up, while we "belted" out whatever melody our hearts needed in the moment. Other drivers may have caught a glimpse of our contorted faces and believed we were suffering a stroke. Waving happily at any such concerned faces we would watch those faces relax in relief with our waves.

Entering the cemetery, Roger made a request that he be buried in his favorite church suit. He wanted to look his best when family and friends made their final goodbyes. Agreeing with his choice, I so much wanted to reassure him and yet the words wouldn't come. I could only listen and attempt to comprehend what he was experiencing. Looking back, I realize how feeble my efforts were as I was lacking the emotional intelligence that would have served this little man well. He was my teacher in this moment and I hope I was an appreciative student. Meandering through the cemetery proved to be more difficult now, as the portable oxygen tank wasn't very manageable.

As we approached the Woods family grave plot, I gave thought to my own fears and concerns. I had never experienced death and was unsure of the process. It was a process that I really wanted to comprehend, believing the better my understanding the more adept I would be in supporting my son with his process. Today, I realize that our remarkable bodies take care of us even as they begin shutting down. My somewhat limited understanding tells me that the circulatory system begins to shift the blood supply to all the major organs in the early stage of dying. This because we are hardwired to survive and by pooling the blood to the major organs rather than to the tips of the toes, the heart, lungs, brain, digestive tract, kidneys, and liver are maintained. This is when people begin to feel cold and seek the comfort of a warm blanket. Death may still be several weeks away, and is stalking the ill person. As the body temperature drops a degree or more hands and feet will feel frigid. (Our little children with Cystic Fibrosis would already have an appearance of being cyanotic but that appearance would deepen tenfold.) The nail beds turn blue along with the lines around the mouth. Ultimately, the blood shifts again, moving away from the digestive system so that the patient then stops feeling hungry. They no longer feel any delight with a favored food. The bowel sounds will be slowing down, maybe even stopping. There is absolutely no point in force feeding people when they've reached this point. It might bring the family some measure of comfort believing they are still serving their loved one, but the patient doesn't require the nutrients any longer and the feeding may actually bring them more discomfort. The breathing now becomes rapid, the respiratory rate slows, and heart beats can become erratic. As this happens death may be just hours away. According to my understanding euphoria now sets in. The body is taking care of the dying mind while the dying mind is taking care of the dying body, and I believe the spirit is very present to the process. Apparently the chemicals known as serotonin, dopamine and norepinephrine continue to increase in the dying process bringing the person the euphoric feeling. I believe the breathing stops first followed by the heartbeat stopping last.

Our walk this day was a short one and over quickly. I concluded a treat would be nice. "Would you be interested in an ice cream from the Dairy Queen I inquired?" Grinning widely, Roger quickly agreed. The day was warming up and a refreshment would be welcomed. As we began our drive home, I asked Roger if he had any other stops in mind. Laying his head back onto the car seat, he let out a long sigh and said he would like to go home and hold his baby sister. I delighted in watching Roger with Cynthia. As he held her, it appeared he was attempting to plant everything about her into his memory. He would study her tiny features, toes and fingers. As she grasped his finger with her tiny hand and held on I realized an eternal bonding was taking place. Goodness and mercy were definitely showing up in our lives.

Chapter Ten

GIFTS FROM THE HEART

The sun was hiding it's brightness behind a ribbon of billowing clouds. From his bedroom we could smell the stuffed bell peppers Stan was baking in the kitchen. Explaining to Roger that his pediatrician would be stopping by soon to change his IV that had infiltrated, I asked if he felt like eating. He explained he had some feelings of hunger but would like to wait for the IV change. We were ever so grateful for our doctor. He was clearly invested in Roger's well-being and cheerfully ran by our house to check on him rather than have Roger wait in his office for an appointment. The gift of his visits truly emanated from a very caring heart.

As I reflected on Roger's current need, my mind wandered to my corridor of memories. A few weeks earlier the doctor was with Roger and myself in this bedroom. The IV's were infiltrating more often these days as his veins were becoming weaker. I had been holding Roger's arm steady while his doctor carefully chased a vein to insert a heparin lock. Finally connecting with a vein, we both realized at the same moment that the cap to the lock was not within our reach. With this sudden realization, I caught a glimpse of my father standing in Roger's doorway. He had arrived with a plate of cookies for Roger as his gift for the day. Noticing he looked unusually pale, I also realized my father who was an incredibly powerful man in many ways had a most startled look on his face. Before I could ask him for help, he quickly stated he would be back later and made a rapid retreat. With no other option I let go of Roger's arm and quickly grabbed the cap. Before we were complete with the wrapping of his arm to protect it, Roger was suggesting that I should check on his pappy. His understanding heart was also very considerate. I continued to reflect on my father's actions and slowly came to realize how difficult it was for him to see his grandson suffer in such a manner. Having been stationed at Pearl Harbor when it was bombed he must have experienced many sights that would haunt him for a lifetime. He was "tough" in so many ways. I had watched him use his pocket knife to pierce his thumbnail that was swollen and blue from having crushed it out on the rig. Clearly his heart was easily pieced when it came to his grandson's suffering.

Having read that it takes forty three muscles to frown and only seventeen muscles to smile, I have become all about conserving energy. I've also been told that the greatest way to feel better about yourself is to do something for someone else. Reflecting on Roger's final days I find myself smiling and feeling amazed as I give thought to his "Secret Pal". A few months before Roger's death, we began hearing knocks on our front door. Oftentimes we opened the door only to find a box with gifts in it. The bearer of the gifts had disappeared from sight! It was fun to share with any visitors that their knock sounded similar to our phantom knockers! With those knocks, Roger's train village began to grow as the gifts included additional cars to add to his train and models for him to put together. The models included a bank and a library to add to the main street of his train village.

Recently I took a picture of our three year old granddaughter in a long pink gingham dress with a white apron and matching bonnet. The dress has the cutest knickers to wear beneath it. In her arms, she holds a cloth doll that has golden yarn curls peeking from beneath her bonnet. She is dressed in a matching gingham dress. The dress and doll were gifts from our secret pals. We have a picture of our little Cynthia wearing the same dress while embracing the cloth doll. It required a skilled seamstress to sew such a delightful gift.

We still have the metal tractor as well as the carved wooden vehicles left by our very talented and gifted visitors. Our grandchildren delight in hearing stories about these generous people who came and went from our doorstep like phantoms, never to be seen. They had to have amazing skills as they made their way out of our yard and into the night. While a variety of gifts including books, which we continue to treasure, were left for us it was the love behind those gifts that lingers with each one of us.

Family members and friends continued to make appearances in our home offering whatever support they believed was needed. Our home teachers were especially supportive, bringing humble spirits into our home with their arrival. One of my brothers had served in Viet Nam. He would arrive late in the evening after a strenuous day at work. Offering Roger some of his military patches, I happily sewed them onto one of Roger's jackets. This particular brother would fall asleep on our sofa, encouraging me to awaken him when it was his turn to sit with Roger and watch his IV and offer whatever measure of comfort he could. He had also encouraged me to use a long broom stick to wake him up, advising me that he might "come up swinging" if too startled. I was grateful for this admonition! And I wondered what dreadful experiences he might have had overseas that would cause such a reaction. Imagine our grief when he would have to face the loss of his beautiful daughter Mazeppa who had brought joy to many of our lives. Mazeppa had been named after our maternal grandmother and had the work ethic of our mother. When we moved from Farmington she was always delighted with our return visits. Gratefully, she had three children by the time she was taken from us in a dreadful accident. Each one of them have blessed our family with their intelligence, humor, and good will.

My brother Patrick would stop by on his way home from visiting his girlfriend who was completing her shift at a fast food restaurant. She was able to send us a bucket of chicken occasionally as it would otherwise have been tossed. Unfortunately as a child, this brother had to have his right arm partially amputated due to the negligence of a doctor. My brother was seven when he broke his arm and I took him to the emergency room as my mother was at work. I was only sixteen at the time and didn't realize that the doctor had placed a cast over an open wound resulting in gangrene attacking his arm and partially destroying the tissue. Years later when I was working for the grocery store I would sometimes be called to the dairy aisle to "control" my mischievous brother. Patrick delighted in entertaining people and he loved to juggle eggs with his one arm, drawing quite a small crowd of admirers.

Early one Saturday morning, the dawn was barely breaking when I awoke to the strangest swishing sound that I had ever heard. It came and went with a steady rhythm. Suddenly, voices began calling out to Roger from his CB radio. "Roger Dodger, can you step outside and wave to us?" Gratefully Roger's oxygen tubing was long enough to make this possible. Can you imagine our delight as we hurried out the front door to discover beautiful "Easter eggs" floating gently above us? We also heard several voices calling out to Roger, wishing him a happy day. Once again, life was coming to Roger and our family in a most fascinating way. The morning sky was lit up with beautiful shapes and colors of balloons waltzing across a blue background. Roger was delighted with his early morning visitors, grateful that in the midst of their exhilarating experience they had thought of him. While Roger would never be able to experience a ride in a balloon, Stan and I eventually would. The feeling is intoxicating as the balloon gently lifts into the heavens, carrying its passengers along at the speed of the air-current. Infinitely gentle, the balloon ride promises a quiet thrill while floating above a city, a desert, a lake, a fragrant meadow or a dense forest of trees. When Stan and I became the chase crew for a balloonist, we found that the morning flights promised dawn panoramas with spectacular sunrises that were magical and amazing! The view from the balloon had the appearance of Roger's miniature train village. We would eventually have the opportunity to fly from locations in scenic Sedona, Arizona, Albuquerque, New Mexico (which was a huge rally), Monument Valley, and tether in small communities in the Rocky Mountains.

Abraham Lincoln once stated, "Most people are about as happy as they make up their minds to be". Early on it appeared Roger had made the decision to be happy. His smile was infectious, his humor unbridled and his love unconditional. One of the beautiful characteristics of young children is their ability to live in the moment. Not being pre-occupied with past problems or future events, they don't bother to crowd their present with worry or regret. Roger had reason to worry with his health failing, and yet he understood the concept that all the worry in the world is not helpfuland does not make a bit of difference.

Chapter Eleven

SACREDNESS IN TEARS

Eventually the day would come when Roger would call me into his room. He was ready to be released from his frail body. He was almost twelve years old and weighed less than forty pounds. As he removed his oxygen cannula, Roger stated, "I'm so sorry mom". We cried softly together and I realized it was time to let go. Stan and I wanted to allow Roger to remain within our home for his final days. But that wasn't possible. Cynthia would need continued care and we needed medical personnel to help us. Making that final drive to the hospital was almost unbearable. But Roger had taught me an important lesson. Courage wasn't the absence of fear. Courage is facing the fear and walking through it. It was in the early morning hours of a brisk November day when Roger drew his last earthly breath. His petition to a very loving Heavenly Father had been granted. He died exactly one year after the release of Cynthia from the hospital. He was incredibly grateful for the year he had with his baby sister. Remembering the words of Viktor Frankl was very helpful to me. He wrote, "We cannot, after all, judge a biography by its length, by the number of pages in it; we must judge by the richness of the contents. Sometimes the 'unfinished' are among the most beautiful symphonies".

Remembering Roger's final days, I recall a tender story that was told over the pulpit on a bright Sunday morning. A woman had received a phone call from a friend telling her that a tragic accident had occurred. Unfortunately several of this woman's family members had suddenly been killed in a horrific car accident. Grief can be paralyzing. Plane reservations would have to be made, suitcases packed, small children tended to, and other tasks completed before the family could fly to the city in which the funerals would take place. As the woman felt over-whelmed with grief and confusion, a neighbor showed up on her doorstep. Having heard the heart wrenching story of the accident, he explained he was there to clean shoes. Stating it had taken him hours to get his family members shoes cleaned for the funeral of his father, he wanted to be of some small service to this family suddenly brought to its knees. This woman learned an important lesson that day. Rather than call and say, "Let me know if I can be of help", be creative and willing to think of one specific service you can provide a grieving family. We had so many services provided us as we planned Roger's funeral it was apparent that many people felt prompted to step forward and respond graciously and thoughtfully to our loss. Someone even remembered Roger's little dog and chose to offer her attention and love, realizing she also would feel the pain of him being suddenly taken from her.

A few months previous to Roger's death I had received a phone call from a very dear friend. She was sobbing and explained that her lovely young daughter had just drawn her last breath. Several weeks previous to the phone call, her daughter had been admitted to the hospital in Albuquerque for a "spring cleaning" just as we were leaving the hospital to take Roger home. She was what was considered a "healthy cystic" and was expected to live into her twenties. Her hospital stay should be short and she would return home to her parents and sisters. This telephone conversation was certainly one that I hadn't expected to be having. As I completed my conversation with my friend, I felt tremendous grief for her and her family. I also believed I understood what they must be feeling. I had much to learn.

While I learned there is value in attempting to enter someone else's world and offer empathy, I cannot possibly know what they are truly experiencing. Each individual person has his own history, perceptions, teachings and understandings. I find it very valuable to remember this important lesson and never say to someone, "I know how you feel".

With the pain and grief that came with the loss of our first born I realized how much grief my friend must have been experiencing when she called me several months previously. I had been worried that my first response to her news, which was to begin sobbing with her, had been thoughtless. Now I realized that I had entered her world and had shared her pain with her. A condolence card that I received after Roger died had some very powerful words of wisdom handwritten in it. The words were spoken created by Washington Irving sometime back in the 1800's. He had penned, "There is a sacredness in tears. They are not the mark of weakness, but of power. They are messengers of over-whelming grief and of unspeakable love". There were many tears shed at Roger's funeral by family and friends alike. We remain eternally grateful for each and every tender act of mercy shown us. And for the people willing to cry with us.

Per his request Roger's marker has the words from one of his favorite hymns on it. We chose the words, "I Am a Child of God" because Roger understood the principle contained in those words. He truly understood that to be a child of God does not mean one is an elitist. For Roger being a child of God meant he was called to accomplish a very difficult mission and in that calling he remained very aware of the need to rely on a loving Heavenly Father.

Chapter Twelve

LIFE IS A HALLOWED JOURNEY

When the Lord commanded Adam and Eve to multiply and replenish the earth he also commanded them not to partake of the fruit of the tree of knowledge of good and evil. They were promised that eating from the tree of knowledge would eventually result in a change to their bodies and that change eventually would lead to their physical death. When they received the commandment to multiply and replenish the earth, they were in a transitional state, no longer in the spirit world but with physical bodies not yet subject to death and not yet capable of pro-creation. They were reminded that they could choose for themselves. What a quandary. To fulfill the commandment to multiply and replenish the earth, they had to disobey the commandment regarding the fruit. As one studies carefully the journey of Adam and Eve, one can truly understand that mortal death was planned for in the councils of heaven. Adam and Eve were warned of the challenges they would face on earth. Because Adam and Eve chose to do what needed to be done, their use of agency allowed man to be. Also, it is important to note that as they traveled a most difficult journey they learned to re-establish communication with Heavenly Father through respectful prayer. Imagine how saddened and alone they must have felt before seeking Heavenly Father through prayer. Because they needed and wanted continuing direction and blessings from their Father, they prayed and then they waited upon their Father for further light and knowledge.

Then they were taught to pray with sincere hearts, with real intent, and with all the faith of their very being. Just as Adam and Eve were taught about prayer, we are also exhorted in Jacob 3:1 to "Look unto God with firmness of mind, and pray unto him with exceeding faith, and he will console you in your afflictions, and he will plead your cause, and send down justice upon those who seek your destruction". It has been my experience that as we pray with sincere hearts, healing thoughts will come, gliding in on the wings of that prayer.

Our Heavenly Father is omnipotent and has all the power needed to control our lives. He truly can save us from accidents, illnesses, protect us and deliver us even from death. With this understanding, I realize that Heavenly Father will not intervene in many instances because we benefit when we experience disappointments, temptations, sorrows, and suffering. Without these opportunities, we cannot grow spiritually. As we recognize life as an eternal process stretching from the pre-earth past and on into the eternal post-death future, then all experiences may be put into a proper perspective. Did I rejoice when our son died? Absolutely not! Was I looking forward to the death of our daughter, realizing that she would die at a younger age than her brother Roger had? Absolutely not! Is the admonition we are given in Proverbs 3:5 "Trust in the Lord with all thine heart", something we know and understand by the age of eight when children are baptized? Indeed not. There is comfort in realizing this life is designed for our growth and progress. I have been assured many times our trials will not be more than we can handle. I have also learned the "rest of the story". If we are to be able to endure to the end we must learn to trust in God while experiencing the trials. Also, as we continue in our journey having a desire to learn and grow spiritually we will blessed with adversities. At times, we may falter in our desire for opportunities; it is then we must pray for further desire in order to receive further light and knowledge. And it is of much value to remember we chose to come to this life siding with Christ's plan rather than Satan's plan in the premortal existence.

I do not intend to indicate that our struggles are not real and difficult! Paul is one of my favorite apostles in the New Testament. His life speaks of incredible struggles and determination whether he was involved in persecuting Christians or joining them in their crusades. Born into a devout Jewish family in the city of Tarsus, Paul inherited the legal advantage of holding the privileged status of Roman citizen. Paul's father being a member of the ancient tribe of Benjamin initially named his son Saul, after Israel's first king. It would be later in life that Saul became known by his Roman name, Paul.

Early on Paul had the privilege of studying under the most respected rabbis in Tarsus. Following the example set by pious Jews, Paul scorned the pagan religion of the majority of the people of Tarsus. Unlike most young Jews however, he was attracted to Greek culture which was the prevailing culture in the near east at this time. As a result of his studies of stoicism, Paul became determined to be governed by the power of reason. Upon reaching the age of thirteen, Paul left home to live with relatives in Jerusalem where he would now have the opportunity to study under the famous rabbi Gamaliel. Because he was a Pharisee, Gamaliel was a member of the Sanhedrin, the Jewish high court.

With his zealous personality, Paul felt obliged to defend the purity of his faith against the Hellenists of the Christian sect in Jerusalem. Eventually he grew in his determination to prove the preachers wrong and would engage in stinging debates in the synagogues and on Jerusalem's streets. Being especially infuriated by the controversial preaching of the Christian Stephen, Paul supported the arrest and stoning of Stephen. Following Stephen's martyrdom, Paul became one of the most active leaders in the bitter persecution of the people engaging in the new faith. At this time many disciples fled Jerusalem to escape the ongoing persecution. One has to wonder if it was at Stephen's stoning that Paul began to realize his heart was in the wrong place. He certainly could not have felt peace and contentment as he heard little children cry for their Christian parents whom he was so bitterly persecuting. Surely their pain was beginning to sink deeply within his soul.

Damascus was a busy commercial center and the Jews became alarmed as they heard reports of Christians who were becoming active there. Paul sought permission from a high priest to travel to Damascus with his sole purpose being to arrest followers of Jesus and bring them to Jerusalem for trial. Paul was supported in his aspirations and would make his journey with a caravan journeying on foot or by donkey. However, the Lord had other plans for him. As the caravan drew closer to Damascus, Paul experienced a vision that would become a conversion experience for him.

That vision is recorded in Acts 9. Drawing close to Damascus, Paul found himself encircled in a light from heaven. As he fell to the earth he heard a voice extorting him, "Saul, Saul, why persecutes thou me?" Paul was quick to respond inquiring, "Who art thou, Lord?" And the Lord said, "I am Jesus whom thou persecutes: it is hard for thee to kick against the pricks". And Paul trembling and astonished responded, "Lord, what wilt thou have me to do?" He was then admonished by the Lord to go into city where he would be advised what he must do. Arising from the earth, Paul realized he could not see and so he was led by the hand into the city of Damascus.

Traveling three days without sight, food or drink, Paul finally arrived in Damascus. A disciple named Ananias had been directed by the Lord to bless Paul in that he would receive his sight. Immediately upon receiving the blessing something like scales fell from Paul's eyes and he regained his sight. Overwhelmed by his amazing experience Paul requested that Ananias baptize him. It was a priesthood miracle that restored Paul's sight and softened his heart! Paul joined the disciples of Jesus who were preaching in Damascus. We are told in Galatians that Paul did take some time to go into Arabia to prepare himself spiritually. Apparently he required support in learning the gospel, just as we all do.

Before long he was preaching in the synagogues, proclaiming that Jesus was the Son of God. All who heard him were amazed, wondering how the man who had made such havoc in Jerusalem could have so profoundly changed. Refusing to believe that Paul was sincere, a number of the people plotted to kill him. When Paul heard of the murderous plot he was able to escape the wrath that was building against him and after being lowered down the wall in a basket by other disciples he fled from Damascus to Jerusalem. While in Jerusalem, Barnabas believed Paul's story and brought him to Peter and James. Eventually Paul would join Barnabas in Antioch.

Over the years Paul would continue his travels, finding humble people from the lower classes and slaves who grasped his message of Jesus more readily than the philosophers of Athens. On one of his missionary journeys Paul was so successful that the temple priests noted a steep decline in pilgrims. The merchants and innkeepers complained of a loss of business. The magicians and healers were especially alarmed as they usually did a brisk business with the pilgrims. Reluctantly, Paul realized he would have to leave the area he was teaching in or face dire consequences.

Paul did face dire consequences several times being imprisoned and/ or flogged for his commitment to Christ. He could have refused to undergo a flogging through invoking shelter under the privilege of being a Roman citizen. That action however could lead to excommunication and his being cut off from admission into the synagogues. He would never allow such curtailment to his missionary efforts however. In spite of the ongoing persecutions, Paul remained determined to carry his message with love and compassion until the day came that he was beheaded. His Christian friends reverently carried his body and head to a nearby cemetery for burial.

I found the apostle Paul to be a most fascinating study. His testimony of our Savior was a powerful example of a true follower of Christ. Paul's life was indeed a hallowed journey. And it serves as a reminder that sooner or later each of us must face our Heavenly Father as recorded in Romans 14:1, for "every knee shall bow and every tongue confess" that Jesus Christ is the Lord. Paul did make a prophetic statement to Timothy just before his death stating, "I have fought a good fight, I have kept the faith, I have finished my course". Contemplating Paul's life after the death of our son, I came to realize each person, young or old has the opportunity to live a hallowed life through the development of knowledge and love for our Savior and through staying the course.

Chapter Thirteen

HUMILITY AND REVELATION

Within a few months of Roger's death, I found employment as a checker for Safeway Groceries. I had worked for the Safeway Stores before and felt such gratitude that I could return to this job as needed. This employment was such a gift in that I could work evenings and week-ends, so that Stan would be available to care for Cynthia and Dennis. He would arrive home from work to find dinner and two excited children to greet him as I made my way out the front door.

Early one Saturday morning, I awoke feeling very startled. I continued to experience dreams that had special meaning to them. While quickly reviewing my schedule for the day a thought continued to intrude on my planning. It was becoming apparent to me that I had to speak with Stan regarding my increasingly frequent visits with these particular promptings. It appeared we had a decision to make that required divine guidance. Realizing that revelation is an intensely personal process and we may receive it through several different conduits, I suggested to Stan that he join me in seeking an understanding regarding our daughter Amanda, whom I believed was still very eager to join our eternal family. I felt that together we needed some kind of confirmation that my dream was revelatory in nature. I did feel my motives were pure in desiring the blessing of a healthy baby and I continued to believe in this possibility. At the same time, I realized it was very difficult to avoid being self -willed in this regard; and I truly desired to be in harmony with God's will. Concluding we would remain prayerful, I went about my business of living life. Explaining to Stan I was off to run errands I quickly left our home.

It was a beautiful clear morning where a chorus of birds were calling out to each other. As I left the driveway from our home, the Holy Ghost clearly spoke to my mind, "fasten your seat belt". Quickly dismissing the thought I continued on my way. We were not encouraged "back in the day" to wear seat belts and I was obviously in denial when the Spirit encouraged me a second and then a third time to fasten my seat belt. (Some of us do have a tendency to need a bit of a slap up the side of the head before we pay attention to divine promptings.) As I approached the stop sign, I concluded it would be wise to listen and then followed through with the prompting, hooking my seat belt rather reluctantly. I was barely half a block into the next street when another vehicle slammed into the side of my car. As my car came to rest upon the curb, I felt alarmed for myself and the driver of the other vehicle. Unable to open the door on my side of the car, I undid my seat belt, slid across the seat and began emerging from my car. Several good Samaritans had stopped to offer their support. Standing erect, I quickly stated I was unharmed. Fortunately so was the driver of the other vehicle. She was rather elderly and I believe turned into my lane not realizing I was beside her. It was then

I realized I could have been seriously injured had I not listened to the repeated promptings. This experience reminded me that receiving revelation can be a very rich and varied process. In this instance the spirit had to almost shout at me as I went about my day very pre-occupied with the tasks at hand.

Gratefully I was able to exchange insurance information with the other driver and I quickly returned to our home. I would discover several days later that I had a whiplash when I awoke and was unable to raise my head from my pillow. Seeking the support of a chiropractor it would take weeks to overcome the whiplash. This is a minor example that is shared in order to stress the understanding that one of the primary purposes of this life is to learn how to receive, recognize and then respond to the voice of the Lord in a timely fashion.

Reflecting on the reoccurring promptings regarding another pregnancy, I again turned to the scriptures. One of my favorite female role models in the scriptures is the very courageous and humble Abigail, a woman whose frequency was truly "tuned to hear". Her story is found in 1 Samuel Chapter 25. It begins with David, a simple shepherd, finding favor with King Saul. We are told that Saul had lost favor with the Lord and his mind had begun to experience deep depression. He appeared to be bordering on the edge of madness. This was due to the fact that the spirit of the Lord had departed from him and an evil spirit was tormenting him. In 1 Samuel 16:16 we are told that Saul was directed to seek out a man who "is a cunning player on a harp: and it shall come to pass, when the evil spirit which is not of God is upon thee, that he shall play with his hand, and thou shalt be well". Saul directed his servants to find him such a man. One of the servants told Saul about David, son of Jesse who was considered cunning in playing a musical instrument. Saul sent for David and young David played on a harp, Saul was refreshed and was well, and the evil spirit departed from him. Saul came to love the young David and appointed him his armor-bearer. David also continued maintaining his job of feeding his father's sheep at Bethlehem.

As David was tending his flock in Bethlehem, Saul and the Israelites had gathered to do battle against the Philistines. Three of David's brothers were in Saul's army. For forty days a Philistine giant had stepped forward to shout a challenge to the Israelite army. He challenged them to find a man who would come up against him. And if that man were able to fight and to kill the giant, then the Philistines would become the servants of the Israelites. And the Philistine said, "I defy the armies of Israel, give me a man that we may fight together".

Eventually David's father sent David with some parched corn and ten loaves of bread and ten cheeses encouraging him to check on his brothers who were in Saul's camp. As David did as his father directed and approached Saul's army, the giant Goliath stepped out of the Philistine lines to shout his challenge to the army of Israel. Saul and the Israelites were very dismayed and frightened. Not one soldier in Saul's army dared to answer Goliath's challenge. David was curious and intrigued asking: "Who is this uncircumcised Philistine, that he should defy the armies of the living God?" Then disregarding the warnings of Saul himself, David ran quickly into the battle line to meet the Philistine. Imagine the amazement everyone present experienced when the young shepherd quickly brought the huge warrior down with a stone hurled from his sling. He then speedily ran to the fallen giant and taking a sword, cut off Goliath's head. With his victory David quickly became a national hero.

As David enjoyed his current status, Saul grew distrustful, suspecting David of having an ambition for his throne. He created plots in which he wrongly surmised that David would be killed. Saul finally promised his youngest daughter to David in marriage with the impossible task of David killing 100 Philistines. David once again proved to be victorious and killed not only 100, but 200 of King Saul's enemies. Unfortunately, King Saul's determination to rid himself of David grew stronger. It appears Saul was falling deeper and deeper into evil and continued to withdraw further from the spirit. In time, David was driven out of Saul's courts and would be denied the opportunity of access to the tabernacle and the rituals of sacrifice. While David would experience the opportunity to kill Saul, he did not pursue this course. He was a wise man in that he understood an important priesthood principle regarding having loyalty to those called by the Lord to preside, even when they may not function perfectly in their calling. While David realized Saul was not succeeding as a king, he knew that it was the Lord's responsibility to remove Saul, not his.

In his exile, David was captured and shortly thereafter released by the Philistines. He then fled to the cave Adullam, near the border between Judah and the Philistine's territory. There a small army of men began to gather around him. This small army included men who were in debt, distressed or discontented. Some of them had deserted from Saul's army. They were a spirited band of rebels always roaming from one camp to another while keeping one step ahead of Saul. They depended on the hospitality of local shepherds and farmers for food and water, growing in number as they roamed the rocky Judean hills. Soon David began to demand tribute from the settlements in the hills in return for the protection he offered them.

Nabal was a wealthy man of Carmel (one of the settlements in the hills). It appears he was a bit of a fool, as David showed favor of him and then asked him for reciprocity for his act of mercy. Nabal in his foolishness not only refused to pay tribute but also chose to mock David! In my estimation, no one in his right mind would choose the course Nabal chose; he sealed his fate as he chose so foolishly. Insulted and infuriated, David (being somewhat impulsive in my estimation) began a plan of action to march against Nabal.

In verse fourteen of 1 Samuel 25, we learn that one of Nabal's young men told Abigail (who was Nabal's wife) about David's plan to march on their estate. This young man demonstrated great courage as he would have lost his life had Nabal learned of what he did. For Nabal would have quickly engaged in battle with David rather than submit meekly to David's demands. But the young man knew that this was a fight not worth fighting and he did what he could do to prevent it.

Abigail is described as "a woman of good understanding and a beautiful countenance". In her wisdom she concluded that she must intercede for her foolish husband. She was willing to humble herself and bring the offense upon herself for her husband's sake. Imagine the blood that would have been spilt had she not understood the dilemma and chose not to intervene. Unbeknownst to Nabal, Abigail approached the outlaw David and offered him grain, bread, wine, raisins, figs and five dressed sheep. Humbly apologizing for the miserliness of her husband, Abigail's quick action saved her household. David responded to Abigail's plea telling her, "Blessed be the Lord God of Israel, which sent thee this day to meet me: and blessed be the thy advice, and blessed be thou, which has kept me this day from shedding blood, and from avenging myself with mine own hand". Clearly David recognized that Abigail had kept him from shedding blood and most likely wiping Nabal and his entire settlement out.

Abigail was an honorable woman preserving the integrity of her marriage. She averted the potential disaster and wisely refrained from sharing the news with her husband upon her return, realizing in his drunkenness he might respond unwisely. Abigail knew full well the principle that there is a time and a place for everything. However in spite of her best efforts to save her husband, when he was sober the next morning and she explained what had transpired, his heart died within him and he "became as a stone". I'm imaging that Nabal might have suffered a stroke or heart attack because of the shocking news he had received. It appears to me that Nabal died emotionally and spiritually first and then died physically days later. There is wisdom in realizing we are spiritual beings having a physical experience in this life. As we feed our spirits, we are more likely to make healthy decisions for our physical bodies.

Upon hearing the news that Nabal was dead David rejoiced. He praised God, realizing that he had been kept from doing evil and the Lord had "returned the wickedness of Nabal upon his own head". David then sent servants who communicated with Abigail. She was advised that David would have her for his wife. Listening to David's servants Abigail was quick to respond, bowing herself to the earth, she replied, "Behold let thy handmaid be a servant to wash the feet of the servants of my Lord". Gathering supplies, Abigail went with the messengers of David and became his wife. I heard it once stated that humility is the cloak in which great men and women wrap them-selves. Abigail was truly a great woman.

It is also noteworthy to point out that Abigail was an exceptional woman in many other ways. One might consider her as a 'type' of Christ. I suggest her loving actions and kind heart brought to David both spiritual and physical sustenance saving him from the sinful heart he had developed, a heart that burned with rage. Just as our Savior continues to soften our hearts as we seek his support. Not only did Abigail save David from sin, she was also seeking to atone for the errors of her husband who was a negligent, self-serving man. This was made clear when she pleaded with David, "Upon me let this iniquity be". Thus she saved two sinners from acting out!

While we didn't consider it a simple matter to bring another child into this world we did consider it a matter that had to be presented to God and not be treated lightly. Reading about Abigail and understanding her humility supported me in realizing the need to listen to the spirit and follow the promptings Stan and I received rather than be concerned or fearful of the judgements that might come from people who didn't understand our journey.

Chapter Fourteen

TO EVERYTHING THERE IS A SEASON

Life continued to remind me that daily hope is vital. Believing that we would have a healthy daughter gave us the confidence needed to pursue another pregnancy. I want to emphasize how hard this decision was for other people to hear, family and friends alike. It must have seemed like insanity to most of the people we knew. I continued to remind myself that we had prayed for something very appropriate and had together received a confirmation.

"Oh no!" I called out to Stan as I emerged from a fitful sleep. It was still early and he had been looking forward to a "lazy" Saturday morning where he would slowly emerge from his cocoon of peaceful rest. Deep within myself, I felt pain like I had never experienced. As a young child in Wyoming, my brother and I had been cautioned by our parents to never enter the field where the Brahma bulls were kept. To be gored by one of them meant a certain and very painful death. As I wrestled with what was happening, I wondered if this is how it felt to be gored by a bull. Continuing to feel panic, I attempted to leave the bed. This was when I realized I must be experiencing a miscarriage.

Stan and I understood this could be a possibility. I had been experiencing some spotting, cramping and lower back pain. Stan immediately placed a call to my gynecologist's office. Because it was a Saturday morning, Stan was instructed to drive me to the emergency room. Feeling anguish, I complied with his directions and threw on a robe. Arriving at the emergency room, I was quickly admitted to the hospital, being advised that I would require a dilation and curettage. We were told this is done to remove tissue in the uterus. While explaining the process to us, my gynecologist emphasized how easy it would be to "tie my tubes" while I was under the general anesthesia. All that was required of me was a signature on a form. I cannot describe fully how angry I felt. To pressure me while I felt so vulnerable was unconscionable! Fortunately my mind was sound enough that I refrained from kicking my doctor as he stood over my gurney and explained "what could be done". I quickly shared again with him that we had a daughter named Amanda waiting to join our family and as soon as I knew she was on the way, I would sign his papers! Heaving a deep sigh this physician patted my hand gently and reassured me that he would do all that was needed to make another pregnancy possible. I truly believe he was genuine in his concerns.

It would be several hours later that I would awake to find myself in a private room. Looking over at Stan I asked him how everything went. He explained that the procedure went well and I could return to our home once I was alert enough to make the drive. Stan also stated that the anesthesiologist would like to show me his hand before we headed home. Feeling puzzled I asked Stan what that was about. He hesitated to answer my question, turning to leave the room in search of the man who wanted to speak with me. A short time later, a man whom I had met just before my procedure walked into our room and inquired how I was feeling. Believing he wanted to be sure I was ready to go home I quickly stated I was "just fine". It was then he held up his hand which had my teeth marks clearly implanted on it! Feeling flushed with embarrassment, I apologized for his injury. This also explained why my neck felt so painful; apparently he had to work hard to disengage my hand without breaking my neck! With a smile on his face, he apologized for my sore neck and appeared to be wearing the same expression of embarrassment that I felt. I had to wonder if in his training he had been warned to watch out for "frantic" patients such as myself.

As we drove home from the hospital, I had unanswered questions that Stan could not help me with. We both were experiencing a sense of confusion. We had not lacked clarity regarding the promise of another daughter who would be healthy! However, we had been advised by the doctor that apparently my body had spontaneously aborted a very sick fetus. Realizing we must not give up hope we both agreed to continue nourishing our moments while seeking further understanding. Also we would have to opportunity to once again experience patience. When Elder Neal A. Maxwell had visited our son Roger shortly before his death, he had advised us that we came to this life to learn patience. Also it is my understanding that the word patience is used about 125 times in the scriptures. There was obviously no point in my stamping my foot, becoming petulant and demanding instant results!

With this plan I knew I had to develop an attitude that would permit me to look forward to the day-to-day routine of caring for my family.

As I reflect on the movie Never Ending Story and the boy attempting with all his might to pull his horse from the Sea of Despair I realize how important it is when experiencing despair to put one foot in front of the other. With renewed resolve I determined to cultivate hope based on recent promptings and allow myself the pleasures of a good book, companionship of friends and family, a good movie, (we had been encouraged by our pediatrician to see Star Wars and that began our weekly venture out to the movies). Stan had a talent for making fry bread that was deep fried in oil (a Navajo friend and co-worker had taught him well) and we agreed it was time for Navajo Tacos. We had established a tradition when it came to this meal. I would cook the beans and meat; Stan would make the fry bread. He would also fry up sopaipillas that we would engorge with honey for dessert. There is always something to focus on that can bring one a sense of satisfaction.

Determined to search for laughter and joy, I continued to watch the television show entitled "Kids Say the Darndest Things". Art Linkletter was the genial host of this sitcom and developed his talent for the ad-libbed into a joyful adventure with children. Then there was Lucille Ball who clearly knew how to use ordinary circumstances to create a very comical sitcom. One day while using my hand mixer, I somehow managed to catch the fingers from my free hand in the mixer while it was running. With both hands fully engaged, I was fortunate Stan was close by and able to unplug the mixer for me. Cautiously removing my twisted fingers from the mixer I told Stan to just call me Lucy because I was obviously as accident prone as she was!

Stan and I both felt a need for the quiet serenity of the mountains as we realized that it is in quiet places that the veil is often parted.

It was also encouraging to notice that our Savior would go into the hills to knock on Heaven's door. Driving from the high desert into the Rocky Mountains was almost intoxicating. One could smell the aroma of sagebrush while enjoying a visual feast of junipers, pinons and eventually the majestic ponderosa pines. Pulling off the highway onto a scenic view, we were amazed when a large buck plunged down the steep side of the mountain. There was a small river meandering beneath the pull-off and he appeared to be headed straight for it. Stan then laughed and reminded me of the first time I had seen a buck in the wilderness.

It was our first winter together and his entire family went deer hunting. The women and children would hang around the campground working on crafts (that particular year ornaments were being made for the Christmas tree we would later venture out and cut). Stan informed me I could hike up the side of the mountain with him if I was up for a chilly early morning adventure. Looking forward to the promise of some real excitement, I quickly took him up on his offer. We walked for what seemed like forever to this city girl when Stan stated, "This is the place". Pointing out a large fallen tree, he invited me to have a seat in this peaceful corner of the world. Pointing out a clearing on the other side of the mountain he stated, "If you see a deer in that open space let me know".

Several hours crept slowly by and I was beginning to feel restless when I spotted movement in the field he had pointed out. Excitedly I shouted, "Look at that huge jack rabbit bounding across that field". Stan moved quickly, bringing his rifle up to his shoulder. Then I heard the loudest explosion! Well, what can I say....this was my first experience hunting and the wildest animal I had ever experienced was the jackrabbit from the panhandle of Texas. Stan was quite amused with my mistake in spite of the fact that I had failed to tell him about the deer until it was almost out of the clearing. Years later we would be out in the woods hunting for a Christmas tree with our daughter Cynthia. After spotting a deer she turned to her father and very deliberately stated, "How can you ever shoot Bambi's mom?" It was definitely a challenge that he took to heart. He would put his rifle away and never hunt again.

As I reflect on this season of our life together, I am reminded of the biblical passage found in Ecclesiastes chapter three. In this chapter we are reminded that "to everything there is a season". The "everything" would include a time to be born, a time to die, a time to plant, to heal and to build up. Of course much more is mentioned in this chapter of Ecclesiastes; we realized we were in a time and place needed for healing and building up. Much of our healing would come from studying and pondering the scriptures individually as well as together. By so doing we would add a dimension to our life that one cannot get through any other means. Our faith would be increased and we would enjoy further understanding and inspiration. Also attending church regularly would allow us to enjoy spiritual intimacy with one another and with Christ.

Chapter Fifteen

BLESSINGS REALIZED

Our daughter Amanda was born on a beautiful spring morning. As a result of the promptings I had felt I was confident she would be a healthy baby. Several hours following her birth I allowed the doctor to tie my tubes. Before her birth I had come to realize through careful study of other people's lives the Lord will often test us and then leave us for some time to learn and grow before granting whatever blessing we have been seeking. Elder Neal A. Maxwell stated, "To be tried really means to be developed which will happen if we are meek, the trials being part of spiritual isometrics". It continues to be clear to me that we benefit in remaining grounded in both patience and faith as we wait upon the Lord for desired blessings. And for some of us this is no easy task!

Cynthia and Dennis were so delighted when we finally brought Amanda home. I had stayed an extra day in the hospital because of my surgery and the children couldn't wait to meet their new baby sister. Cynthia pulled her little rocking chair up next to mine and carefully unwrapped her baby doll. This was the beginning of a completely new experience for us. She would catch on quickly to breast feeding and was happy to show visitors how this was done. Explaining to her that grown-ups already knew how to feed babies she relented and stopped giving that lesson. Her interest in her baby sister never waned however. She was eager to help with the bathing, rocking, and diaper changing of the baby, cooing to her as she participated in all the "fun". She never questioned why her baby sister didn't require inhalation and physical therapy however. She just seemed to have an intense desire to savor every moment with Amanda. Observing the excitement in Cynthia's eyes I realized how much gratitude and fulfillment I had felt during the seventeen months Cynthia had been in our home. She was bubbly, outgoing and so in love with life. Her locks of shining blonde hair and her blue eyes were a perfect combination!

"Mama, tell that brat to leave me alone!" Apparently Cynthia was feeling impatient and frustrated with her little sister Amanda. Her words of impatience were music to my ears. Our two little munchkin girls could "break up and make up" at least once a day. Sometimes it would be of benefit to offer assistance and other times, it would be best to allow them their own space. In this instance I would continue to focus on the task at hand realizing by Cynthia's tone that she was just expressing her frustration.

I did however choose to investigate when I heard the two girls sitting at the bottom of the stairs that led into the family room later in the day. They were giggling and shrieking at the same time. Starting down the stairs, I inquired as to what was entertaining them. As they answered and I drew closer, I was startled to see two very large scorpions dancing just beneath their feet. I quickly moved from being a hovering helicopter to an exterminator. A scorpion bite could be deadly to Cynthia.

I have corridors filled with memories of these two girls and their antics. Santa Claus had left them a Barbie jeep one year beneath the Christmas tree. They were squealing with delight as they scrambled to take their places in the two seater. Cynthia quickly advised Amanda she was "too young" to drive and therefore she would be the passenger. Chuckling over their current power struggle, I was determined to "wait and watch". Throwing on her sunglasses Cynthia said she would drive Amanda to the place where she could get a driver's license. This appeared to appease Amanda's state of agitation as she withdrew her sunglasses from her little bag and climbed into the passenger's seat. And off they went down our driveway with Cynthia coming to a complete stop at the bottom of the drive before continuing her journey. We lived on a dead end street and had minimum traffic during the day. Back to hovering like a helicopter I was on the lawn ready to leap into the street should I be needed.

Life with two daughters is enchanting and magical. We had a fairy garden in our backyard that included many "gentle people". Several attempts were made to create a fairy castle made of sand. Gratefully, our carpenter aka daddy, came through and created a delightful and rather whimsical home for our magical creatures. Our fairies had wings that were alive with every color of the rainbow. Sunlight danced on shimmering wings as the fairies dipped and flew with the butterflies. Imagine our delight when two magnificent mythical unicorns made their appearance. It was no surprise to me that these creatures of purity and grace joined us in our adventures. Our imaginations delighted in creating these mythical creatures and they would capture our attention repeatedly. I was a bit cautious of handling the lizards that the girls would allow to hang out on their shoulders. I suspect Dennis was the instigator behind the lizard escapades.

Stan was quite the athlete whether he was snow skiing or water skiing. Amanda and Dennis were his shadows. Cynthia and I were the people in the ski lodge sipping hot chocolate and enjoying a panoramic view of the glistening, frosted mountain from our warm and comfy padded chairs. Our entire family enjoyed the local skating rink. One of our friends with cystic fibrosis would skate around the rink with Dennis at her side. He would be carrying her oxygen for her and was very careful to maintain the same pace she did. Dennis was gifted in maintaining his balance, and we never worried that he would trip and cause his friend any harm.

We had a number of children on our dead end street and after school the neighborhood would spring to life. We also had Lena Mae. She was the unofficial spy with a powerful determination to maintain her stewardship as the only "grandmother" on the block. She would bring boundaries and dimensions to our neighborhood that only a seasoned grandmother can bring. Realizing that children are extremely sensitive to adult attitudes, Lena made serious attempts to remain firm when directing the children while avoiding any semblance of being dominating. Her soft spoken voice became the voice of reason and encouragement to many of the children. She and her husband Bill also had the prettiest yard, raising amazing roses and lilac bushes. One day Cynthia appeared from her playroom with her "southern belle" dress on. She had also dressed Amanda. She informed me that they would be crossing the street in order to visit Lena's rose garden. Chuckling to myself I offered to be the doorman and as I helped usher them down the steps I felt immeasurable love for Lena. Her genuine interest in the little munchkins emanated from a very gracious heart. Every neighborhood with children would benefit in being blessed with a "Lena".

Cynthia's favorite meal was liver and fried onions. I have no memory of how this meal was introduced to her but I do know that she "required" it several times a week. Awaking early one morning she requested this meal. She also wanted to have a tea party and invite her friend Noel. Within a few hours we were on our way to purchase the liver and special treats for the tea party. As a cute young teenage boy was unloading our groceries into my very unsightly pinto station wagon Cynthia turned to me and stated, "Mom next time we need to bring the Mercedes". She and Amanda would then whisper and giggle all the way home.

There were numerous trips to Anna Kaseman Hospital in Albuquerque for Cynthia. During one stay the hospital staff was enjoying celebrating Halloween. A "body" was laid out on a gurney for example. Covered with a "bloody" sheet all that could be seen was a pumpkin head. The hospital staff dressed for the occasion as well. Cynthia and I were standing at the nurse's station when a very tall and imposing "Darth Vader" came through the double doors. I've never seen a little girl disappear behind a desk as fast as Cynthia did dragging me with her. As Darth approached she refused to budge an inch. Feeling remiss at creating such a fright for her the staff member attempted to reach out to her. Realizing she was not to be coached out of her fright he quickly left the unit. Opening the desk drawer, a very thoughtful nurse handed Cynthia a piece of candy and stated, "Wow...that was close!" Everyone started laughing and Cynthia resumed her position at the corner of the desk, keeping a watchful eye out for whatever might happen next. She would not be disappointed as Raggedy Ann and Andy danced through the door throwing kisses left and right.

The parade of characters would continue throughout the course of the day bringing delight to everyone's heart.

One year previous to Cynthia's death I had the opportunity to attend a workshop in Santa Fe, New Mexico. It was a hospice workshop and Dr. Elizabeth Kubler Ross was the featured speaker. She explained during the course of her lecture that if you have a dying child, ask them to draw you a picture. She emphasized it would need to be a simple request with no hints of your desires. Continuing to explain, Dr. Ross stated, "dying children are living on such a spiritual plane they know the time and date of their death".

It would be several months later that Cynthia was once again admitted to the hospital in Albuquerque. By now Cynthia's breathing capacity had become very limited. She was required to wear her oxygen cannula continuously. Her veins had become so "used up" that she had to have her IV placed in the back of her hand. In spite of these limitations, she would have me style her blonde hair and dress her in her cute clothes and then place her in a wheelchair. With her oxygen cart in one hand and guiding her wheelchair with the other, we would then stroll down to the end of the hallway where a large picture window allowed a view of the glorious New Mexico sunset. Cynthia greeted each visitor coming into the hospital as classical music was being piped into the area. The setting was so peaceful and Cynthia remained engaged in enjoying the beauty of Heavenly Father's world. She knew the value of sharing her joy with others.

As she was feeling bored one afternoon, I made a simple request. Suggesting that we always loved her art work, I asked that she draw me a picture. On our return home, I tucked the picture into my scriptures where it would remain over these years. Each time I examine the picture I continue to be amazed at its accuracy. It not only has the date and time of her death, the picture also includes nine balloons. The nurses who had the day shift had returned that evening with helium filled balloons and explained to Cynthia that if they could give her anything it would be healthy lungs. In her picture, there are two little girls with the number 9 on one's t-shirt and the number 7 on the other. The one with the nine is holding 8 balloons in her hand while the 9th one is hovering in a corner of the room. As the nurses released the balloons to float above Cynthia's bed, one left the bunch and drifted to the corner of the room. Cynthia's birthday was only a few days away and she would turn 9. Amanda's seventh birthday would happen the following April. I chose to believe that Cynthia would live to Amanda's seventh birthday. She in fact died on October 9th at 7:00 AM.

Chapter Sixteen

A PROPER PERSPECTIVE

Shadows wrapped her hospital room in darkness as Cynthia lay upon her pillows struggling to breathe. Several folks had dropped by the hospital in Albuquerque to pay their respects and say a final goodbye within the past two days. Cards with cute drawings and loving words came in the mail. Our neighbors from Farmington, Bill and Lena had cautiously crept into her room just after lunch. Bill stood over her and appeared to be struggling as he laid his hand upon her tiny back and spoke words of endearment. Lena was unable to speak.

My brother Mike had driven Dennis and Amanda to Albuquerque the day previous to her death. He also brought a dear friend from Farmington with the friend's puppy that was several months old. Cynthia had been so excited when the puppies were born and had claimed one as her own. As we laid the puppy beside her pillow, Cynthia stretched out her hand to pet it. The puppy began licking her hand and then curled upon it, remaining there for some time. It was amazing to see this little puppy remain so quiet and still with her.

As Cynthia began moving into the final hours of her young life, I was gently rubbing her back and thinking to myself. I was wondering where my youngest brother might be stationed. He was in the Special Forces and I knew he would want to be appraised of Cynthia's passing. Imagine how startled I felt when she raised her little head and questioned, "Where is Uncle Ernie mama?" She was somehow hearing my thoughts! He would explain to me years later that his life has been saved on two different occasions by his little niece who had become his guardian angel. Our Cynthia was an angel in the shape of our daughter.

"Tell that lady I'm not ready yet!" Imagine how startled I was as Cynthia raised her head from her pillow and appeared to be glaring at someone in the corner of her hospital room. This would happen a few hours before she became comatose. I realized that someone was there to take our little one to her eternal home. I didn't know how to respond. Suddenly I realized I didn't have to. My job was to remain present to our little munchkin. After a few minutes, she raised her head and stated, "Mama put me in the van and take me home." Motioning to Stan's sister to sit beside Cynthia, I asked Stan to come out into the hallway. Explaining that I understood what she meant when Cynthia asked me to place her in the van, I told him she wanted us to take her body home to Farmington when she died. We were not to leave her in the hands of strangers in Albuquerque. It took Stan a few minutes to comprehend what I was saying. As he pondered the request I went to the nurse's station and explained to them what we planned to do. Cynthia had her favorite blanket with her. I wanted to wrap her little body in it and honor her request by driving her home ourselves. The nurses stated we would need a death certificate in order to transport her body. They appeared willing to support us in our needs. We placed a call to the funeral home in Farmington and advised them we would need to bring our little one to them sometime within the next twenty four hours. They were willing to be there for us. Stan's sister Sharon stated she would like to make the drive with us. I was able to reassure Cynthia that we would take her home when the time came. With this news she quietly moved into a place that she would not return from. Stan would later find a note from her in his scriptures with the words of the hymn "Abide with Me" on it. "When other helpers fail and comforts flee, Help of the helpless, oh, abide with me". Her faith had not faltered as she struggled with her disease and subsequent death. It appeared Cynthia would have us increase in our faith rather than falter.

We had so many amazing experiences over the years with Roger and Cynthia. Family, friends and church members remained active in supporting us through dark days when it appeared the sun might never shine again. Learning to maintain a proper perspective through this journey with our children I was especially grateful when I read the words of an anonymous poet:

"Pain stayed so long I said to him today, 'I will not have you with me anymore'.

I stamped my foot and said, 'Be on your way!' And paused there, startled at the look

He wore. 'I who have been your teacher—all you know of understanding love, of

Sympathy and patience, I have taught you. Shall I go?' He spoke the truth, this

Strange unwelcome guest; I watched him leave, and knew he was wise. He left a heart grown tender in my breast. He left a far, clear vision in my eyes. I dried my tears and lifted up a song."

Cynthia's class members at her grade school planted a tree with a plaque beneath it in her memory the year following her death. We were so touched with their kindness and continue to visit the tree when we are in Farmington.

Chapter Seventeen

A MOTHER'S LOVE

"I hate you", Amanda screamed as she tore through the front door, rushed past me to her bedroom door and slammed it shut. Returning home from school that day must have been especially hard for her. Our family had taken a few days off after Cynthia's death to just be together. Then we realized we had to "get back into the saddle". Alarmed with Amanda's fury I went to her door and could hear her crying and throwing things. Speaking to her through the door, I asked would she let me know when we could talk. Finally she cautiously opened her door; I remained still allowing her to speak first. She was sobbing uncontrollably and it was all I could do to just be still. Then as she began to regain her composure she stated, "I was waiting on the playground and Cindy didn't come to play with me". Again the tears were flowing. "And I hate you because you wouldn't keep her alive!" Oh my. I was not prepared for this. Entering her painful world, I acknowledged my limitations and her grief. Then we cried together.

It would take weeks for our lives to return to a normal routine. Amanda and I agreed to share some of Cynthia's stuffed animals and books with her friends. We would sort and then re-sort. I wanted to be clear that Amanda supported the choices that were made. Dennis would sometimes be consulted. This was a time for healing and each of our family members were hurting and struggling. My mother had died suddenly the year previous to Cynthia's death. I came across some of her belongings that I wanted to send to siblings. There was wisdom now in completing business and moving on. Visiting my mother's grave I contemplated the words on her marker:

"A mother's eyes reflect the love of Heaven, A mother's hands reflect a life of service, A life of sacrifice for those she loves, And with her giving hands, She shapes the soul of man, Prepares him for eternal life above."

Mother was an amazingly courageous woman who raised nine children. She loved people and enjoyed meeting and working with others. She was a woman who would not let her struggles define her. She had also been suffering with migraines for many years. Suddenly her headaches were stronger and fiercer. One day she called and asked me to drive her to the hospital. On the drive she began removing her jewelry and asked that I make sure specific family members received specific pieces. I was so startled. Asking her what she thought was wrong, she just reiterated her request. She had been vomiting violently while experiencing a horrific headache and I assumed she had a very severe flu. Imagine my dismay when she was admitted to the hospital and I remembered a conversation we had had months earlier.

Mother had asked to ride with me to the clinic in Albuquerque for Cynthia's check-up. After a few hours into the drive, Cynthia began to doze off. Mother took this time to share with me that she believed she had a brain tumor. I was in total denial. She was barely sixty years of age and mothers are supposed to live forever!

Arriving at the medical clinic I reassured mother that our appointment wouldn't take long. Cynthia was weighed and measured. Following that routine her physician quickly joined us for her examine. Gratefully we wouldn't be kept waiting an endless amount of time. Much to our dismay Dr. Goddard examined Cynthia and revealed she was experiencing bronchial breathing; she would have to be hospitalized immediately. We were all three startled with this news. It had sometimes been difficult for me to determine Cynthia's needs and I felt saddened that I hadn't realized we were headed into a hard time for her. Mother agreed to spend the night in Cynthia's hospital room with us and I would drive her to the bus depot early the next morning for her return home.

This would be the first time that mother would experience the physical pain of Cynthia's illness. Blood gases would have to be drawn. As the lab technician entered her room, mother explained to Cynthia that she would just be waiting in the hallway. Cynthia was quick to object. She wanted her granny to hold her arm still for her as they would do the draw from her tiny wrist where the artery was. While I could see that this was so difficult for mother she remained and supported Cynthia in her need. The night was long and arduous. Cynthia and I had spent many nights like this together; it would be my mother's first and I could see how difficult it was for her. She had been given a cot to sleep on and I would sleep beside Cynthia in her hospital bed. Mom's sleep was fitful and I was really concerned for her when I left her at the bus depot early the next morning.

Cynthia and I returned to Farmington several weeks later. Upon our return mother was suddenly very busy and seemed to be avoiding me. I didn't understand her reluctance to spend time with me. Questioning her about the possibility of a brain tumor, she advised me she had seen a physician who had given her pain medication for her migraines and she would be fine.

It would be several months later when she would call and request that fateful ride to the hospital. Following mother's admission to the hospital I had to return home as Stan was away on a business trip and Cynthia needed her therapy. My sister Billie agreed to check on mother early the next morning. Almost immediately upon her arrival she called me to express her alarm. She had arrived to find mother unresponsive. Advising her to alert a nurse, I made arrangements for a friend to come and tend the children. Rushing to the hospital I recalled my dream from a few weeks earlier. In my dream I had seen a woman with a swollen body receiving emergency care. My fear was mounting. As I approached my mother's room, I glanced quickly into the doorway. A code blue had been called and hospital staff were surrounding her bed working on her. I instantly recalled my dream and realized this was what it had been about. I quickly read her chart. It stated she had fallen out of the bed in the night. Immediately I went in search of our pediatrician. Gratefully he was on the pediatric unit completing his rounds. He came quickly to mother's room, read her chart and suggested we call in a neurologist.

A short time later a nurse advised us mother was being taken for x-rays. Because I was so familiar with the lay out of the hospital, I eased myself into the room where several medical personnel were discussing mother's x-rays. They were startled when I spoke quietly from the darkness, asking questions that I felt were pertinent to her care. I was advised she either had a brain bleed from the fall or she had a tumor. The neurologist scheduled her for surgery advising us it would be lengthy, complex and the outcome uncertain. Returning to her room, I began calling family members.

Within hours the waiting room was filled with her children. Eventually a very kind neurologist had the difficult task of informing us that she had a brain tumor pressing on her brain stem. Should she survive the surgery she had just experienced she would possibly be paralyzed. They had placed her on life support and our task now was to speak to her individually and watch the brain monitor for any sign of activity. The hope was that she would recognize our voices and be able to respond. We also called local priesthood leaders to give her a blessing. As they approached her bedside to offer the blessing, I retreated to a corner of the room. My siblings surrounded her bed and I believed they would need the comfort of hearing the blessing. As I bowed my head and closed my eyes, I felt hands upon my head and the most incredible divine love flowed through my entire being. I knew then that all was well with my mom. She didn't recover consciousness following her surgery and we gathered to plan her funeral.

Chapter Eighteen

STRONGER AT THE BROKEN PLACES

During the difficult years with our children, Stan's health problems and mother's brain tumor, recalling the words of Hemingway was helpful. He concluded that everybody is broken by life, but some people are stronger at the broken places. My resolve to do something with my life experiences grew as I contemplated the next chapter of my life. I wanted to choose a course that would ensure I would grow stronger rather than "fold". Considering the stages of grief, I realized they were similar to that of a person who is beginning a path to recovery from addiction. For example denial is often the first stage of grief and addiction followed by anger, bargaining, depression, and eventually acceptance. Gratefully a friend had introduced me to a family therapist following the death of our children. I had experienced severe depression with Roger's death and while I managed to continue functioning, the grief counseling offered me an opportunity to rebuild my shattered emotional life. This began my journey to emotional healing and a fulfillment of my life calling. Returning to school I was able to begin an internship at Suncrest Psychiatric Hospital in Farmington. My goal was to become an addiction counselor.

With that internship, I found the study of family systems to be fascinating. Life had been difficult for myself and Stan; there were times when I wondered if we would remain together. Those times came when we had been stretched emotionally, physically, financially, and spiritually. As I learned about the dynamics of a healthy functional marriage, my concern for our relationship began to be diminished. We had chosen to stand by one another no matter what. We had been wise in making the Lord our advocate; this decision was essential to the health of our relationship.

I also appreciated an invaluable truth that the eternal destiny of each person resides in his or her own hands. Each person in a committed relationship is responsible for his or her own healing, actions, happiness and his or her own spiritual growth. And there are times when a person may find themselves lost in despair, depression, anxiety, or sorrow. Should that time come, they may require a hand up. As I mentioned earlier, C.S. Lewis's faith had a profound effect upon his writing. He believed that we become who we are through many choices, large and small, over time. Illustrating this principle in a little book called "The Great Divorce" Lewis acts as the narrator on a bus ride from Hell to the outskirts of Heaven. Along the way he describes little vignettes that teach important lessons. One conclusion that Lewis draws is that all who choose wrong roads perish; he points out, "their rescue consists in being put back on the right road".

Lewis was also clear regarding agency. One of my favorite stories that he wrote involves Lucy. As the story unfolds, Lucy is concerned about the predicament of a band of Dwarfs as they have become very self-absorbed. Eventually Aslan (who is the Savior figure) teaches Lucy that the Dwarfs have chosen cunning rather than belief. Because of their lack of faith and subsequent fear they have created a prison in their own minds. As Lewis so succinctly demonstrated, the Dwarfs made an active choice to live in self -deception. They were exercising their God given agency.

Gradually I began to understand the concept of agency in regard to addiction. A person who becomes addicted to anything including alcohol, drugs, pornography, gambling, etc. has subsequently limited their agency. Of course, that person didn't deliberately set out to self-destruct. I considered it a privilege to be of assistance to anyone seeking support in getting back on the right road. Realizing that substances and behaviors can diminish a person's ability to feel the spirit, I felt excited with my new journey as I would have the opportunity to teach truth. And with that truth, support people in becoming stronger at their broken places.

As I began serving my internship and pursuing college courses that would support my credentialing, I entered a world that I would sometimes find absolutely staggering. I learned that the road to recovery is not a straight, upward climb for people. Oftentimes a person would take several steps forward and then a step backward. Others would be like the polar bear confined in a very small holding cell at the zoo. Realizing the cruelty of that holding cell, money was raised and a new habitat created for that polar bear. Where he had paced back and forth endlessly in a very small area, he was now surrounded by an immense space as his bars were lifted and his new lodging made available. Unfortunately, the polar bear was stuck within the confines of his well patterned brain. Rather than risk moving out into his new space he would continue his pacing back and forth along his old path. He would have to be coaxed out into his new spacious habitat. Just like the polar bear, recovery from addiction meant connecting with patterns, then correcting any pattern that was self-defeating.

In my studies I also learned that in dysfunctional families most members have greatly impaired freedom due to the toxic shame that binds each member. Like the polar bear, the family members have created patterns of living that inhibit freedoms and creates considerable emotional pain. Rather than finding joy in the journey of life these family members find anxiety and depression. Understanding and separating the difference between toxic shame and guilt meant truly understanding toxic shame. In my pursuits I learned that toxic shame refers to painful humiliation, heightened embarrassment and diminished sense of self. In that state of despair a person learns to hide their thoughts, feelings and hopes. They have an image that must be maintained at all cost. Therefore the creation of a mask to hide behind becomes imperative. Or course, each individual is very creative in developing their mask. They learn what brand of clothes are acceptable, what model of automobile to drive, what vacation spots are most desirable.

I have several family members and friends who have flown to Europe to vacation. While my friends and family members have delighted in sharing pictures and experiences, they have been appropriate in their sharing. However, I once observed a woman describing to a harried department store clerk her experience while traveling in Europe. This particular woman was too involved in maintaining her image to even notice how her sharing was affecting customers who were quite ready to get on with making their purchase. She was also obviously a high achiever and probably a workaholic. She would be very invested in her community as well as her circle of friends. However her hidden core of shame would cost her authenticity and genuineness.

In a nutshell, healthy guilt tells me I have made a mistake through violating a personal value and I can correct my mistake, avoid repeating it and forgive myself for being a vulnerable human being. I will also have an honest desire to make restitution for my mistake, if possible. Toxic shame tells me I am a mistake leaving no room for restitution or forgiveness. How can a person ever find true peace if they are bound by their mistakes and have no real understanding of the repentance process? Once a person develops a shame bound identity, the core of that person's life is so painful that out of sheer desperation they develop unhealthy coping skills which may lead to one or several addictions.

The pathway to recovery involves much risk taking. It can also be very relieving to stop that internal dialogue that demands perfection and tells me I have to succeed in order to have any value or worth. It's my belief, shared by many others, that a word we would benefit in dropping from our vocabulary is "should". I had transported clients to a speaker's meeting when I first heard this suggestion take place. The speaker began explaining that her worth had been bound up in her productivity and she had begun to build resentments regarding her weaknesses and inability to always perform at her very best. Continuing to explain, she had begun to realize through her attendance in meetings that she was "shoulding" on herself daily which meant continued feelings of ineptness and a lack of gratitude for the many talents she had been given. I marveled at her openness and humility as she shared with humor and compassion her understanding of toxic shame.

It is a reality that children can make themselves intrusive and obnoxious in any social setting. Recall the last time you were in a restaurant or supermarket and you observed children displaying deplorable manners. Perhaps they were your children. If your family lives within the walls of a respectful family system, you will be able to see your children and other children as separate beings, on their own journey of discovery. Rather than condemning the children for their rude behavior you will use the experience as an opportunity to teach them respect for others. Through avoiding any form of condemnation or shaming, the young people won't be belittled or made to feel less than. Honoring their stewardship, as a person shapes the souls of the little ones placed in their charge, it is very helpful to remember the scripture found in Luke 18:16. "But Jesus called them unto him, and said, 'suffer little children to come unto me, and forbid them not: for of such is the kingdom of God.'

Realizing that everyone has experiences that have changed their mental pair of glasses, my journey would now teach me to live more fully and happily. I came to realize I could easily enter another person's world and understand their feelings, then make a quick retreat back to my own. For example, when my mother had called me to drive her to the hospital, as soon as I entered her presence, I felt the headache she was describing. That headache wouldn't leave me until I left her at the hospital. When my brother Mike had knee surgery and was experiencing considerable pain, I entered his hospital room and nearly folded from the sharp pain I was experiencing in my knee. I was finally beginning to understand that my spirit and intellect could resonate with someone else, I could have emotional empathy, "stand" in someone else's shoes and quickly return to my reality. Gratefully this gift of empathy would serve me well in the field I was called to.

Courage is best understood when it is painted boldly in the life actions of a person. On our journey with Roger and Cynthia, we were amazed at their courage and the courage of other children suffering with cystic fibrosis. Little did we realize that our son Dennis would be faced with a life that would often call for courageous actions while he was being faced with very difficult challenges? He has been faced with an illness that creates a pain and suffering which is almost indescribable. I firmly believe that the severe mood swings of bipolar disorder are quite unimaginable to those who have not suffered it. Add anxiety disorder to that mix and you have a mixture that creates a terrible black cloud of despair. As I entered the field I had no idea that what I was about to learn would be used to support our son Dennis. I would come to realize that if you are diagnosed with a terminal illness such as cystic fibrosis or cancer you eventually beat it or you die. With mental illness, it creates ongoing despair that is consuming enough at times that one might be driven to attempt suicide. Dennis would be faced with the fact over and over again, that he would never get better or recover from his mental illness. At times he would be able to manage his symptoms and at other times he was haunted by voices telling him to hurt himself, that he wasn't worthy of life and that he had been abandoned by God.

Chapter Nineteen

VALLEY OF DESPAIR

Dennis initially collapsed in the front yard of my father-in-law's home at age sixteen. He was well on his way into madness when he was misdiagnosed with seizure disorder. Unfortunately another genetic disease was claiming another of our children. Gratefully both bipolar disorder and seizure disorder respond well to Depakote and phenobarbital. Unfortunately, bipolar disorder incites dreadful behaviors while destroying the basis of rational thought. It can erode a person's will to live. Dennis made his first bold attempt at suicide using phenobarbital.

As a young child I learned that nature is a force to be reckoned with. Living close to the panhandle of Texas assured that our family would sometimes seek the safety of a tornado shelter, following a massive thunderstorm. Oftentimes, tornados would appear on the heels of those thunderstorms. As an adult and living on the west coast, my family has visited a number of inactive volcanoes in the Cascade Range. Lively discussions have occurred with friends as they shared their experiences when Mount St. Helens Volcano erupted in the eighties.

Just like nature, mental illness can either give or take life. The manic side of the disease has been described as a strange driving force. A force that creates energy, enthusiasm and imagination. A person experiencing mania will develop racing thoughts and pressured speech. Their behavior may become provocative and out of character for them. Shyness will disappear and the now persistent provocativeness will become pervasive. Mania can also create despair and psychosis as one becomes wildly out of control, sometimes becoming paranoid and delusional. Dennis's baffling and frightening symptoms began several years previous to his "seizure" episode. With his deepening depression, we thought he was experiencing grief over the loss of his brother and sister and two grandmothers who died suddenly. When Dennis entered high school, he found the energy at the school to be too much for him and we placed him in a private Christian school. Not recognizing he was experiencing mania he would spiral into more deep, obsessive thinking and miss out on much needed sleep. Finally a restful night's sleep would slow his manic thoughts down, reset his cycle and help him avoid a mental explosion.

There is the reality that many over-achievers do suffer from bi-polar disorder while appearing to be highly successful. Identifying bipolar disorder, whether it be bipolar I disorder or bipolar II disorder means understanding that a person with either disorder demonstrates extreme highs which lead to lack of sleep. Eventually the crash comes when the person moves into their depression mode. Unfortunately bipolar disorder in children often gets misdiagnosed. A number of children diagnosed with attention-deficit disorder with hyperactivity are actually suffering from the early symptoms of bipolar disorder.

While being typically overlooked, the behaviors and temperamental features of this disorder can begin to emerge very early on. Sadly bi-polar children can experience periods of explosive rage. They may throw temper tantrums for hours at a time. If chronicity sets in, they cycle back and forth with little relief in between. Their cycles can be rapid, happening more than four times a year. Or they may ultra-rapid cycle within a week or month. Tragically, some may frequently spike highs and lows within a twenty-four-hour period. Early onset bi-polar children may also experience separation anxiety and night terrors. Often their dreams are filled with images of blood and gore. Gratefully, our son did not exhibit these painful episodes.

It's important to note that some children with bi-polar disorder are diagnosed with oppositional behavior disorder when in fact they are children with bi-polar disorder who are experiencing a very diffi-cult time transitioning or complying with a request from a parent or older sibling. They have already imagined an agenda that works for them and any alteration in the sequence may be more than they can handle. For example, initially a mother may tell her daughter that she will take her shopping for the doll clothes she has saved to buy. Realizing she would like to reward her daughter for earning the money for the dolls clothes, the mother surprises her daughter shar-ing that before they shop, they will stop for a treat at the ice cream parlor. This abrupt change could create a meltdown rather than the expected excitement it might bring a child who does not suffer with this disorder. Understanding that children with bipolar disorder lack the flexibility that allows for a smooth transition from one activity to another, it is of much value to learn to prepare these children for any transition far in advance of making it so that they have ample time to prepare themselves. While allowing for more flexibility a parent could be avoiding a war within their own home.

It is my experience both within the walls of my own home as a parent and working with other parents, we do not want to be told we are over-involved or be blamed for being negligent parents. We recently had our doorbell ring at 3:00 a.m. Imagine our confusion as we peered out the peephole and observed a young girl about age seven speaking to the stuffed animal she was holding. I was in my bathrobe and felt comfortable opening the door while Stan returned quickly to the bedroom to get fully dressed. This very precocious youngster was in her pajamas, wearing socks and carrying her stuffed animal and a plastic glass. She obviously wasn't going to leave home without several very important items. As I looked into her oval face framed by lovely dark curls I inquired as to the nature of this very early morning visit. She quickly stated, "I can't go back home. My mom won't quit yelling at me". Speaking quickly with Stan, he and I both agreed we should immediately return her to her home and attempt to learn what had happened that drove her out into the night. She managed to take us to her home as slowly as possible, avoiding the most direct route. As we walked in the chilly darkness of the night, this young lady held tightly to my hand while explaining her plans to be a scientist when she "grows up". Fascinated by her lack of concern in visiting with a total stranger, I asked her if she had seen me in the neighborhood before. She quickly replied, "oh yes, you walk that white dog and I ride my bicycle in front of your house". Relief washed over me as I continued speaking with her, realizing she had sought out the neighborhood grandmother much like our children might have sought out Lena Mae back in the day. As she pointed out her home, she appeared to feel safe in us returning her to her parents. Ringing the doorbell, her father appeared confused upon answering the door and discovering his daughter smiling up at him. He was dressed in pajama bottoms and a tee shirt. As I quickly explained the circumstances this father offered an explanation. His wife was pregnant and was missing her circle of friends back home. He went on to explain that they were attempting to sell their home and move back into the neighborhood they had left behind in San Antonio. I completely understood the dilemma they were faced with. Feeling some relief we handed this delightful little sprite over to her father, and took the short route to our home. As we walked and shared how very strange this experience was, we both agreed we would call the police and have them check in on this family. While making the call, I requested a follow up visit from the officer in order to let go of any concerns that might be lingering in the recesses of my maternal mind. It was within the half hour that we were paid a visit by the officer. He assured us that all was well. The young girl had shared with him that she didn't like her mother yelling at her. He was obviously a parent and responded to the little one's complaint in a parental rather than official manner. "Your mother will probably yell at you a lot more before you turn eighteen and leave home". He appeared wise in his decision not to blame or criticize the parents for having such a bright and self-reliant little girl. He then advised them that they might consider adding a lock to the top corner of their door, perhaps preventing any future escapades into the night. While I do not suspect this young girl had any mental health concerns, I am delighted her parents were not shamed or criticized for the actions of their little escape artist.

It's also important to realize that parents of children diagnosed with bipolar disorder suffer deeply as they begin to realize their dreams and expectations for their child have been dashed against the jagged rocks of an unforgiving coastline. Initially they have typical expectations that with their child they will experience family outings, sports, amazing holidays, high school graduations, and then the opportunity to visit college campuses. Not to mention the courtships and eventual anticipated weddings where everything will be "happy ever after". Dr. Elizabeth Kubler Ross described the "little deaths" that each one of us face daily. The loss of a favorite pocket knife, a favorite book loaned but never returned, a beloved pet, belief in a friend or family member that proves false, opportunity for new employment in a distant community resulting in close friends being left behind, marriage, divorce, retirement, and illness. I'm referring to individual situations of personal growth and change that may include a visit with grief. As suddenly and violently as a tornado or earthquake, bipolar disorder uproots so many hopes, expectations, and dreams. Rather than look forward to the future with exciting expectations, with the diagnosis of bipolar disorder in their child a family may be shaken to its very core and the accompanying grief can be over-whelming. Helping to carry other's burdens through sitting patiently and in silence while someone talks about their depression is definitely what we are taught to do by our Savior. C.S. Lewis stated, "The fact that our hearts yearn for something Earth can't supply is proof that Heaven must be our home". Realizing that no religious group is exempt from the pain and suffering brought on by mental illness is imperative in our society.

There are so many parenting books written and so many experts who have voiced their philosophies on how to reach children and win their cooperation. Parents of a bipolar child will be wise in realizing all the typical parenting skills will be met with incredible resistance by their child. Learning to become the parent this child needs can be incredibly challenging and feel overwhelming. It would behoove such a parent to understand that with the feelings of grandiosity a bipolar child experiences comes huge expectations of perfection. I and others are of the opinion that the anxiety level of these children is so high that they feel compelled to dig in their heels in order to feel some semblance of control. Just as a parent wouldn't insist that a crippled child play basketball, parents of a bipolar child have to modify their expectations and practice patience in the process.

A book that I studied is entitled "The Explosive Child". I took it on one of my flights from Oregon to Texas and was studying and marking pages when a fellow passenger showed interest in what I was doing. He began describing his son and his concerns for the rages that spewed from his son toward the son's mother when no one else was around. He was describing very tough times punctuated by wild rages that could last for hours. Using strategies that normally worked such as sticker charts and time outs had made no impact. I was able to quickly show him a quotation from the book by psychologist Ross Greene; "Consequences can be effective if a child is in a state of mind to appreciate their meaning, but they don't work nearly as well if a child is not able to maintain such a state of mind". Realizing that they would benefit with professional help this father appeared to have a strong commitment in seeking an intelligent solution.

Bipolar disorder in young people can be as lethal as it is in adults. I find the statistics on adolescent suicide deeply disturbing as it is reported as the third leading cause of death in adolescence. Having raised two teenagers and worked the adolescent unit at Suncrest hospital I realize it is almost impossible to second guess what's going on inside a teenager's mind. Common warning signs of suicidal intention (not all inclusive) include depressed mood, increased social withdrawal, changes in appearance including grooming, giving away important possessions, decline in school performance, changes in sleep pattern, use of alcohol and drugs (self-medicating), and loss of interest in previous enjoyable activities.

Seeking answers from our son as I prepared to write this section of my book, I asked him to describe how he remembers his life as a teenager. He stated that there were many times he felt worthless and in turn self- destructive. There were no affirmations, thoughts or prayers that could change those feelings. What would change his feelings was a shift into mania. Then he would have so much energy that he didn't know what to do with it.

Chapter Twenty

LIVE TO LOVE, LOVE TO LIVE

Having experienced the disease that ravaged Roger and Cynthia and observing Stan's journey with kidney disease and colon cancer, I am of the opinion that mental illness is one of the most painful and protracted trials an individual can face. Experiencing depression and anxiety to some degree with Roger and Cynthia's journey I cannot imagine living with a brain disorder that causes mild to severe disturbances in thinking, feeling, perception and behavior. I am of the opinion people enduring mental illness benefit most when nourished with tenderness.

Like so many other afflictions mental illness cannot be dismissed at will and being tormented by a mental illness does not mean a person lacks in personal righteousness. They too are experiencing the refiner's fire and their experiences can be for their good. Maintaining our belief in a loving Heavenly Father who is perfect enables us to truly love ourselves, our imperfect family members, neighbors, friends and strangers.

Peace can flow into our hearts and souls when we choose humility and avoid any form of judgement regarding a person's descent into the valley of despair. We cannot understand what has gone through the mind of a person who has committed suicide while mentally ill or depressed. Only Heavenly Father knows if the person was capable of understanding the seriousness and finality of their actions. Perhaps that person had cried out for help only to have his or her pleading fall on deaf ears. Perhaps those ears were deaf due to a lack of recognition or understanding regarding the desperate person.

Having been an addiction counselor, I have often appreciated the mantra, "An attitude of gratitude". While a person cannot avoid becoming tired or sick, there is wisdom in understanding that gratitude is a vehicle that will carry us along the pathways of affliction while we avoiding getting stuck in ruts of self-pity, despair and feelings of inadequacy. Elder Neal A. Maxwell counseled us to make "quiet but more honest inventories of our strengths". He admonished us to understand that "most of us are dishonest bookkeepers and need confirming outside auditors". We have all been blessed with talents that we may be overlooking.

While facing mental illness or standing on the sidelines of a beloved family members mental illness it would behoove us to realize a great crisis of faith may be lurking just around the corner. Responding to the challenge may mean we seek appropriate professional help while reaching out to church leaders for blessings; we may benefit in exercising faith in both options. It is also imperative that a person continue with their prescribed medication. Through maintaining their medications, a person is more likely to avoid recurrences of their disorder. Unfortunately as some folks begin to experience diminished symptoms as a result of their medication regime, they begin to develop the false concept that they no longer need medication. While medications may not eliminate mood cycling, they do slow it down allowing for milder symptoms between episodes. Hopefully the right medication regime will help resolve an episode that has already taken place, reduce the severity of symptoms experienced in between and delay future episodes while perhaps minimizing the severity of any recurring episode. With this positive experience may come a false sense of security allowing the thinking error that a person no longer needs medication. In answering the question regarding continued use of medications, I want to emphasize it has been our experience with Dennis that even with feeling better, he still requires his medication. This because of the underlying biological predisposition to the illness. Oftentimes when people with bipolar disorder stop taking medications, they relapse and are worse off than before beginning the meds. Unfortunately some people enjoy the hypomania that comes with cycling and are willing to experience the lows. The danger in this of course is where their low will lead them. Some people with bi-polar disorder do not understand the need for prophylaxis-the use of medication while experiencing a period of stability. Cycling is the nature of bi-polar disorder and failure to remain on medication may be mean movement into a very painful and destructive episode.

And family members must always remember they are not alone and avoid isolating or living in anguish. It is also vital that people of any faith avoid false beliefs regarding mental illness. People suffering from mental illness are not responsible for their plight and twisting doctrinal truth must be avoided. The "if only" that naturally follow a mental illness diagnosis or suicide of a person with mental illness can be especially agonizing for parents and spouses. To demonstrate empathy and regard for these folks is to live according to our Heavenly Father's will.

Regarding our personal experience, Dennis's future appeared promising when he was able to acquire a degree in business and find employment in management with a prominent local retailer. He began his career filled with great optimism. Settling into his new employment, Dennis worked very hard and slept very little. Unbeknownst to him and to us, his decreased sleep was both a symptom of mania and a cause of it. Facing each day with excitement he had envisioned himself eventually becoming a buyer for the department store. As he progressed into his illness that dream would be crushed. Initially, he was successfully employed with this company in Eugene, Oregon for a number of years. Eventually the vice president of the company promoted him and he transferred to Boise, Idaho.

Dennis enjoyed the beauty of Boise; finding an amazing bike path that offered him a connection with the outdoors that was exhilarating. Downtown Boise is very inviting with its clean environment and amazing shops. Making friends who enjoyed rafting, biking and hiking, Dennis was delighted with his success and his friends. Life was good and he was content for the most part.

We would drive over from Eugene, Oregon and learn to enjoy this corner of the world with him. Camping at Red Fish Lake, we found the jagged Sawtooth Mountains to be quite different from our experience with the Rocky Mountains and the Cascade Mountains. The Sawtooth Mountains are named the American Alp for good reason, remaining snowcapped year round. The lake that we visited and surrounding mountains are breath taking. If one is especially adventurous I understand there is the possibility of superb backpacking in primitive places. While the lake was charming and beautiful, the mountains were stunningly beautiful with their jagged edges appearing to be razor sharp.

After a successful eight years with this company, Dennis faced a new dilemma. The owner had decided to liquidate and the stores would be closed. Several weeks before the doors would close headhunters from a major chain of retailers sought Dennis out. Feeling relieved as he would now have the opportunity to continue in his chosen field, Dennis didn't understand the demands that would be made of him. Unfortunately, too often in retail, one can leave work late into the night only to have to return with the break of dawn. For a person with manic depression this is a recipe for disaster. It is my belief that in addition to having a strong work ethic, Dennis also experienced considerable mania that was both mesmerizing and exhilarating. He was very creative and inspiring. Unfortunately for him psychological disaster was formulating.

He would be hospitalized twice while in Boise due to mental health issues. Gratefully he received helpful professional care and was able to return to his employment. Back in the 1800's, mental institutions were referred to as lunatic asylums. They served as housing for anyone who was on a journey into Hell and had little or no resources. If you were mentally ill, middle-class and had resources, you might avoid a stay in one of these notorious facilities. Sadly, those who weren't fortunate enough to avoid being warehoused in one of these abominations would most certainly experience electroshock therapy. This form of therapy was routinely administered with portable machines that wheeled were around the units. They were used primarily as a means to create order. While electroconvulsive therapy is used in today's world to treat severe depression when antidepressant medications have been of no use, electroshock therapy has come a long way from the procedures used in the early days. Some psychiatrists who oppose the use of it claim that undergoing the procedure is similar to playing Russian roulette with the brain. Proven side effects include memory loss, cognitive problems, headaches, muscle pain and nausea. Gratefully in today's world the choice to use this particular form of therapy lies with the individual. It cannot be forced upon the individual and written consent must be given by the patient or a court appointed guardian.

Lithium is the gold standard mood stabilizer for many children and adolescents as well as adults. With Dennis's diagnosis of bipolar disorder he was prescribed lithium. Because lithium is almost entirely eliminated from the kidneys, Dennis underwent a kidney function test prior to his being placed on the lithium. After beginning Lithium it was imperative that he have periodic blood tests to determine the level of lithium concentrations in his blood. The concentration must be held within a specific range in order for the lithium to be effective. After many years of being on Lithium the day came when he appeared to need a different medication regime. While we had read conflicting reports regarding the effect on kidneys with long term use, Dennis was beginning to demonstrate some kidney damage. Reading the reports that described lithium treatment as being associated with an approximately sevenfold reduction of suicide attempts and fatalities in bipolar patients, we felt alarmed as we considered his options. Gratefully there are a number of anticonvulsant medications available for the treatment of mania in adults. The search was back on for a reasonable medication that would be an effective treatment for acute mania and the avoidance of any future episodes. Remembering that he had been prescribed an anticonvulsant at age sixteen and the positive results it produced, we were not surprised to learn his psychiatrist was considering the use of an anticonvulsant. The years of searching for the ideal combination of medications for Dennis has helped us understand there is no "ideal" in mental illness.

In spite of the challenges he was faced with, Dennis would continue to remain successful in his chosen field for a number of years while continuing to seek medications that supported his stability. In our journey with Dennis, we discovered that mental illness is common among great people. Winston Churchill was plagued with feelings of hopelessness naming his depressive spells "the black dog". And yet Churchill is counted as the greatest Englishman and one of the greatest souls of the twentieth century. Other notable sufferers of mental disorders have included Abraham Lincoln, Theodore Roosevelt, Ludwig von Beethoven, and Johann von Goethe and Ernest Hemingway. Obviously these amazing men would find means of coping that would allow them to continue in their greatness. Unfortunately many ordinary people have had their dreams crushed and their promising futures have ceased to exist as they began their terrible journeys into mental illness.

Currently, according to statistics from the National Institute of Mental health major depression affects 20% to 25% of adults at some point during lifetime. Their symptoms include disturbance of sleep patterns, which includes awakening early and being unable to get back to sleep. Then there is the lack of energy and interest in anything including food, family or employment. This is also when I believe toxic shame may set in. I have read that the Chinese say the dragon has the power to render itself invisible. Like an invisible dragon, toxic shame is invisible and its claws can literally lock a person into a frozen state. Realizing that toxic shame emerges from a person failing to keep his or her image intact, it's important to understand how much their personal dignity is greatly diminished. It's difficult to imagine how a depressed person can survive a massive shame attack. Gratefully, our society has become more forgiving and very cognizant of the need for support when a person is mentally ill and with that support, quite often toxic shame is not invited to the event.

As I stated earlier, Bipolar Disorder occurs when a person has alternating periods of deep depression and manic euphoria, sometimes separated by periods of normal moods. Psychotic depression is a variant of major depression, but the person develops hallucinations, delusions or both. We were living in Eugene Oregon when Dennis was once again experiencing a major break. Stan was returning to our home for lunch when he found me outside, attempting to coax Dennis down from the fence. Just beneath him was a paved driveway. Gratefully, Stan was driving his pick-up and he backed up to the fence and asked Dennis to hop down into the back of the truck. Dennis initially refused, explaining that "it was part of the plan". It would take considerable effort to thwart his plan, and gratefully Dennis finally became willing to drop into the back of the pick-up. We drove him to the emergency room where he was placed on a psychiatric hold and eventually the correct medication regime was established. This would be his first experience with Lithium. Unfortunately many people are opposed to taking lithium which always leads to a recurrence of their illness. Fortunately, Dennis was agreeable to this plan of action and some semblance of sanity was restored to him. He would continue on his journey for a number of years eventually accepting that he could no longer work due to the cycles that were slowly eating away at his ability to function on his own. Dennis currently lives in our home with us. He contributes daily to our household, having regained his sense of humor as he gained acceptance of his limitations.

According to the National Mental Health Association approximately six million young people in America suffer from a mental health disorder which will seriously interrupt their functioning at school, in their homes and their circle of friends. Unfortunately the majority of young people who commit suicide are profoundly depressed and their loved ones have not connected the dots until it is too late. It is imperative that our society recognize that no one is immune from mental illness. And there is so much available in today's world to support the needs of people who suffer.

My conclusion overall is that we will all be broken by life. It is our Savior's love that dispenses grace and we will do well to turn to him in all things. While Stan and I were just kids when we fell in love, we continue in our "golden years" to grow in love. Our love for one another has evolved through our efforts to keep God in our lives and maintain our Savior as our rock. Realizing the wisdom that is to be found in the scriptures was crucial for us. We have come to understand that no matter what the odds are against us, we will not and cannot fall. This guarantee is eternal. In our golden years we feel prepared for the inevitable day when we will face our own death. William Cullen Bryant obviously had pondered his own demise. He wrote a poem that I continue to ponder. It brings meaning to my life.

"So live, that when thy summons comes to join

The innumerable caravan, which moves

To that mysterious realm, where each shall take

His chamber in the silent halls of death,

Thou go not, like the quarry slave at night,

Scourged in his dungeon, but, sustained and soothed

By an unfaltering trust, approach thy grave,

Like one who wraps the drapery of his couch

About him, and lies down in pleasant dreams".

About the Author: Judy Lloyd was a certified therapist with over twenty years' experience as an addiction counselor. Being employed as an in-patient therapist in a residential program in Farmington NM and an out-patient therapist in an out-patient program in Eugene, OR she facilitated groups and worked with individuals. Previous to her employment, she gained considerable experience in dealing with the grief process as two of her children were born with cystic fibrosis, a surviving son has experienced both bi-polar disorder and anxiety disorder and her spouse has experienced colon cancer and kidney disease. She has served in various capacities in her church including a four year mission with the church 12 step program.